Radical Gratitude

Radical Gratitude

Mary Jo Leddy

ORBIS BOOKS
Maryknoll, New York 10545

Fourth Printing, December 2003

Founded in 1970, Orbis Books endeavors to publish works that enlighten the mind, nourish the spirit, and challenge the conscience. The publishing arm of the Maryknoll Fathers and Brothers, Orbis seeks to explore the global dimensions of the Christian faith and mission, to invite dialogue with diverse cultures and religious traditions, and to serve the cause of reconciliation and peace. The books published reflect the opinions of their authors and are not meant to represent the official position of the Maryknoll Society. To obtain more information about Maryknoll and Orbis Books, please visit our website at www.maryknoll.org. To purchase our books online, visit www.maryknollmall.org.

Library of Congress Cataloging in Publication Data

Leddy, Mary Jo
    Radical gratitude / Mary Jo Leddy.
        p.   cm.
    ISBN 1-57075-448-9 (pbk.)
    1.   Gratitude—Religious aspects—Christianity.   I. Title.
    BV4647.G8 L43 2002
    241'.4—dc21

                                                    2002003645

In Memory of Wilber Sutherland
also called *Amtikaye: Standing on a Rock*
(1924–1997)

Contents

1. BEGINNINGS...1

2. PERPETUAL DISSATISFACTION...............................14
    What Drives Us? 18
    The Culture of Money 19
    The Captivity of Craving 21
    Culturally Induced Dissatisfaction 23
    A Deeper Dissatisfaction 25
    A Wider Dissatisfaction......................................27
    Partial Liberations 29
    Captivity Then and Now......................................32

3. RADICAL GRATITUDE 38
    Stories of Gratitude 41
        My Beginning 41
        Beginning Again, Out of the Great Blue 42
        Christopher..44
        Overwhelming Goodness on September 11 44
        A Preference for Being 46
        The Sun and Poverty.....................................46
        Room Enough for Gratitude...........................47
        Someone to Thank 48
        The Multiplication of Money 49
    The Dynamics of Gratitude 50
    Beyond Dissatisfaction..52
    The Great Economy of Grace 55
    Ingratitude 59

Loving God for Nothing 61

Eucharist 63

Giving Ourselves Away 65

Jesus, the Example of Radical Gratitude 68

Acting on Gratitude 69

4. CREATIVE POWER 71

The Craving for Power 73

Power and Controlling Interest 76

Powerlessness Corrupts 79

Dreams Deferred 81

The Resentment of Powerlessness 82

Powerlessness and Violence 83

The Enchantment of Powerlessness 84

The Innocence of Victims 85

The Organization of Powerlessness 87

Relational Power 89

The Omnipotence of God 93

Real Powerlessness and Radical Powerlessness 96

The Power of Jesus 97

The Power of Christian Community 100

5. THE POINT OF OUR BEING 104

Episodic Meaning 105

Lifelines from the Past 107

The Myth of Progress 109

From Better to More 112

The Empire of More 113

Without a Vision the People Perish 116

Political Ways of Coping with a Loss of Vision ...120

The Future and Class Time 124

Imperial Ideologies 126

The Need for Enemies 128

Living with Purpose 132

Jesus and the Point of His Being 139

6. LIVING WITH SPIRIT 142

    1. Begin before You Are Ready.......................................144

    2. Practice Gratitude..145

    3. Gather with Like-Spirited People............................152

    4. Live More Simply..156

    5. Look for Good Examples 159

    6. Think with the Mind of Your Heart 162

    7. See from the Center and the Edge............................165

    8. Be Connected to a Longer Tradition,
       a Wider Community...165

    9. Find a Beloved Community 168

  10. Contemplate the Face of the World..........................170

Acknowledgments 174

Notes on Sources and Recommended Readings 175

CHAPTER ONE

Beginnings

WE GIVE YOU THANKS

The words wind their way
through the bedrock of centuries
and up through the layers
of ourselves upon selves
tilling, tolling, telling

WE GIVE YOU THANKS

What we say with our words is so much less important than what we mean with our lives. Only our lives give weight to our words.

I believe that each one of us has at least one significant word to say with our lives. This word is who we really are, who we are meant to become, our calling in this world. Within this word lies the secret of our happiness, the source of our power, and the mysterious point of our being. Through this particular word of our lives we bring the one thing still wanted and awaited in the world, the one thing necessary that no other can give. A particular grace.

It is not easy to identify the word, which both concentrates and extends one's life. More obvious to a few, it is usually a long process of discovery for most. Like Jacob we each have an angel to wrestle with, the messenger who reveals our true name which is both wound and blessing.

We may spend years trying to become someone else, someone other than ourselves. The point of our being may become lost in thoughtless determinations. And then there is the noise, the mind-filling noise of our century, that makes it difficult to attend to the still, small word, which longs to grow up and be given.

Still, life impresses.

In spite of ourselves and sometimes because of us, there is a beckoning and a hearkening. At times it comes as a whisper of difference: what if and why not and so be it. Sometimes, all the false notes of our lives strike us, strike us down, until we take a sounding of our soul. There may be a day when someone crashes through the door of our self-contained world, when a problem is left at our doorstep, and we are summoned. There is no one else. This you must do.

There are moments too of unconstructed love and loveliness in which we are found and lost and found again. The impertinence of beauty and the tensile strength of truth startle us afresh, loosening our grip on things.

These are the blessed beginnings, ordinary graces.

I believe that at least once in our lives, perhaps once in a year, maybe even once a day, we are recalled to our true selves and to the meaning of our lives. Such revelations are not rare, not given to only a few. They are given to each of us in generous recurrence. Such invitations can be missed, denied, accepted or rejected. Life impresses but it does not impose.

The time of my particular life has left this impression on me—that I am summoned to gratitude, to become a word, an act, of gratitude. For this I was created, in this lies my happiness. Of this I am convinced, even as I long to understand why and how this is so.

There are many other words I have mentioned with my life, words like justice, faith, love and friendship, peace and care for the earth, but gratitude is the word that moves through and beyond them all. Gratitude is how I weigh-in on the world. It is the spirit that shapes me and folds me into faith.

This book is conceived between two realizations: that I am already grateful and that I am not yet grateful. I am ungrateful in a sadly predictable way and my life does not always give weight to my words. Happily I write this book as much for myself as for anyone else. If this leaves me humble, I trust it will, nonetheless, give the reader a measure of hope.

However, this book also begins with the conviction that it is not meant for me alone. It has something to say, a liberating word—here in America, the North and the West. I use the phrase "America, the North and the West" to describe not only a geographical reality but a state of mind as well. Readers who live in other "Western" countries will probably be able to identify with some of the concerns that animate this book.

It also has something to say specifically now, in the time after September 11. It is still difficult to see through the dust of that day of destruction, to find words beyond mute sorrow or rage. Indeed, we will be sifting through the ashes of that horrible event for many years to come. Some will be tempted to try to get back to "normal" life, to business as usual, to the way things were before September 11. However, there are many more who have been deeply shaken, who are engaging in a profound reassessment of their lives. On the left and on the right, there is an intensified questioning of some of the basic political and economic assumptions that have guided our thought and action. These questions did not begin on September 11. Indeed, they have been with us for some time, but they have concentrated and extended the minds of our hearts.

Such questions, when heard at length and in all their depth, resound as the foundational religious questions, the root (or radical) questions, that lie beneath the surface of the more obvious life of a culture: What is the meaning and purpose of life? Wherein lies happiness?

My own insight is that we cannot rebuild our lives simply by constructing bigger, better, and stronger buildings. We must begin by thinking in a more foundational way, a more radical way. We must begin by becoming grateful.

However, although this book begins and ends in gratitude, it must go by the way of reflecting critically on why it seems so difficult to sustain gratitude as an all-encompassing attitude to life. The difficulty will defy our efforts to resolve it personally, for ingratitude is ingrained in our economic system and in the worldview that has shaped our imaginations for more than 200 years. We have been wasting away for want of gratitude for some time. Gratitude will not come easily here and now—not, or at least not primarily, because we are morally or psychologically weak but because the predominant values of our culture are so subtle and all-pervasive.

There is an argument to be made for gratitude, but I also know that it is neither possible nor desirable to argue someone into or out of a sense of gratitude. Such an attitude can be evoked only in desire, described more than defined. One can learn to recognize it as much in its painful absence as in its sure presence. One can also give good reasons why gratitude is not only personally but also socially liberating. If and when these good reasons coincide with recognition, they can become compelling.

This is not a book about the "spirituality" of gratitude in the trendiest sense of that term, although it is an attempt to recover some of the ancient wisdom about gratitude. It is not primarily about developing an inner attitude, which will lead to a healthier, more balanced personal life, although it will possibly have that as a side effect. And this is not a theological study, although it may invite you to think more about what you believe.

Instead, consider this as an invitation to ponder gratitude as the most radical attitude to life. It is an attitude that dissolves the easy distinction between what is called "spiritual" and the world of "material" concerns. Spirit is not different from matter; it is more than matter. Gratitude arises in that in-between space where the inner and outer worlds meet and touch and encompass each other. Authentic spirituality, genuine politics, and good economics arise from a spirit of radical gratitude.

So impossible this seems. It is more possible to feel so overwhelmed by the pace and magnitude of the changes taking place in the "outer" world that one turns toward changing the only world that one has some control over, the world of the self. This involves an admission, consciously or unconsciously, that one feels rather helpless and powerless in what is happening in the world "out there."

Are we forced to choose then between either claiming an interior form of personal peace and caring for the world at the expense of our peace of mind? Some writers seem to think so. There are indeed books that will offer some advice on how to create a cloister for the self in the midst of this frenetic and fearful world, books about spirituality as a lifestyle. This is not one of them. And there are books that make us feel guilty about such an abandonment of the world of suffering and injustice—but this is not one of them.

This book is about ordinary grace, which is here for the asking. For free. And it is because such ordinary grace can neither be bought nor sold that it is so promising in a time and a place defined by what has been called "the triumph of American materialism." This book is about living an alternative to a driven, consumed, and consuming existence. It is about liberation for those who live behind a plastic curtain, a virtual curtain, in a particular and very perplexing form of captivity that separates us from ourselves and others and from God with a film as impenetrable as it is fleeting. It is about authentic liberation in a culture that is supposed to be the most liberated in the world, that is given over to the pursuit of happiness and is, nonetheless, chronically dissatisfied. It is about liberation for people who seem to live in the most powerful culture in the world but nevertheless can feel quite powerless over many aspects of their lives. It is about liberation that begins with a sense of gratitude for the most ordinary and taken-for-granted realities.

I have written about gratitude from and for the context of North America because this is the "given" of my life, the location of its blessings and burdens. Our insights float into an atmosphere of abstraction when they become dislocated. As good poets and novelists know, thoughts and metaphors and images become more universally accessible to the extent that they are really situated in a certain time and place. My reflections begin here, are rooted here, although this cannot and should not be where they end.

I am aware of the difficulties involved in describing the crux of one's own culture. Culture is like the air we breathe and, like fish in the water, we remain largely unconscious of the context in which we live and move and have our being.

There are, of course, many "worlds" and at least two countries within North America. Inevitably, some of my generalizations will be helpful and others will not. Where you stand gives you a certain understanding. Where you live influences what you see. The people you listen to affect what you hear. My rather modest hope in writing this book is that it will at least encourage others to take a second look at where they are.

In the following chapter, I attempt to describe the "perpetual dissatisfaction" that is integral to an economic system, that expands to the extent that it can continue to expand the needs and wants of consumers. This artificially induced craving becomes a habit of being, perpetual dissatisfaction. I will suggest that this dissatisfaction with what one has expands until it eventually inverts and implodes within oneself, resulting in a profound dissatisfaction with who one is. The centrifugal force of this craving draws everything into the consuming self, which is itself consumed in the process. Thus ensue the pervasive sense of powerlessness and the vague sense of guilt that afflict so many in North America—and this in an age where many have rejected the guilt associated with religion and in a place which is the center of power in the world.

We are held captive by our cravings and by a sense that we are powerless to effect any fundamental change in the world about us. No amount of moralizing about the millions of starving people on this earth or self-conscious exhortations about the virtues of the simple life will break the force and direction of this craving. Liberation from the craving that holds us captive will have to come from a more fundamental shift of attitudes. It is only radical gratitude that will liberate us from this bind, and yet the reasons for such gratitude must also be evoked, unbound, liberated.

The following three chapters describe some of the basic convictions that underlie the possibility of liberating gratitude in the particular North American context of captivity.

Radical gratitude begins when we stop taking life for granted. It arises in the astonishment at the miracle of creation and of our own creation. As "In the beginning," this miracle is more fundamental than anything we try to manufacture or work on. In gratitude, the vicious cycle of dissatisfaction with life is broken and we begin anew in the recognition of what we have rather than in what we don't, in the acknowledgment of who we are rather than in the awareness of who we aren't. Gratitude is the foundation of faith in God as the Creator of all beginnings, great and small. It awakens the imagination to another way of being, to another kind of economy, the great economy of grace in which each person is of infinite value and worth.

Yet, this imagined possibility often seems so vulnerable to the inexorable dynamics of the real world of economics and politics that hold us captive. Do we have reason to hope in a world in which it is a little easier to be grateful?

Gratitude will forever remain a nice and sometimes comforting attitude until and unless we also consider whether or not we have the power to make some changes in our lives and in our world. We will remain captive, as I will suggest, until we begin to question the models of power that dominate our culture and to search for a different understanding of power, one that gratitude liberates and that liberates gratitude. Power is not necessarily destructive; it can also be creative.

We begin to move beyond our sense of powerlessness in changing the world (and ourselves) when we consider the power that grows in the energy of relationships and in the dynamism of our relationship to God. If we are from God, then we also share in the creative power of God. If we are from God, we are also with God, in God. Chapter four outlines how actively relating to the creative power of God liberates us from the economically induced sense of powerlessness that perpetuates our captive state of existence.

Chapter five assumes that our purpose in life is not simply getting more, earning more, being more. The meaning of life, the point of our being, is that we are created for God. Understanding that we are *from* God and *with* God is also to become aware of how we are meant to be *for* God. This seems ever more important in a culture that is losing, or has lost, a common social sense of what it is for. In the absence of an overarching common vision, the goal of getting more has filled this social vacuum. However, even in a culture that has lost a common sense of political purpose, or that has only a negative sense of political purpose, it is still possible to live with a sense of meaning and direction and with some measure of happiness. In the experience of radical gratitude we know the origin and purpose of our lives.

The Trinitarian understanding of God implied in these chapters should now be obvious. It will also be evident throughout these chapters that I take Jesus as the great teacher of gratitude, not only in his words but also in the graciousness of his living and dying.

Chapter six of this book suggests more practical ways of developing the habit of gratitude, of living with spirit. How can we live so that gratitude is not only an intermittent awareness but also a habit of being? Gratitude leads us to action and prayer and to genuine relationships but it is also true that we become grateful by practicing gratitude.

Finally, let me say more about the writer who will doubtless appear in the following pages. I was baptized almost as soon as I was born and I grew up in a world in which Christianity was both familiar and friendly. It is also the way of faith that I have continued to choose. This is the ground beneath my feet, the light in which I see, the tonality of a tradition that has attuned me to the discord and harmonies of life. I cannot imagine the world outside of the words, the concepts, the symbols, and even the fragrance of this tradition. Words like Benediction, Eucharist, and Resurrection come almost naturally to mind, as do idolatry, temptation, and captivity. These words wind their way through the centuries and up through the layers of my selves upon selves. It is perhaps because of this tradition, so expressive of the conviction that "the Word was made flesh," that I cannot imagine any authentic spirituality that leaves the body of the church or the body of the world behind.

I would like to be a disciple of Jesus and I know at times that I am not. Of this I am sure, that I have never been happier than when I took the risk of believing that Jesus meant what he said.

For better or worse, I grew up in the Christian tradition in the very concrete form of the Roman Catholic Church. It is a church as filled with saints as with sinners, like myself, as given to truth as it is prone to error, as much on the side of oppression as liberation. My church has an astonishing ability to be critical of contemporary Western culture and even, occasionally, of itself. Yet, it is also blinded by prejudice, authoritarianism, and petty games of power. It is a church that claims to be more spiritual than political, yet that is, nonetheless, all too political and distressingly dispirited at times. However, the problem is not simply "out there" in "others." It is also in me, as I am a member of this church. In short, this is a church that both reveals and conceals the liberating gratitude of Jesus.

Let me emphasize that my criticisms of certain aspects of North American culture should not serve to justify injustice and weaknesses in the church. This is something that more conservative Christians are prone to do. Their fierce examination of evils in society seems to blind them to the presence of other evils in their church. More liberal Christians, on the other hand, are so outraged by the inadequacies and injustices in the church that they can remain unconscious of the extent to which they have internalized and are held captive by some of the more unfortunate biases of their culture.

I have often been asked why, as a woman, I continue to stay in the church. My simplest answer, and perhaps the truest, is that it sustains me in gratitude. It also makes it more difficult for me to retreat into some lifestyle enclave of spirituality. It keeps me real. The church reminds me that my culture is not the center of the world and that it cannot serve as the sole arbiter of significance. And it has ways of presenting more than it knows about birth and death and all that lies in between. Saving graces. Sacraments.

Some may even wonder why I have continued to use the traditional word "God" to describe the source of liberating gratitude and creative power in our lives. Is there not some better, more meaningful word? For reasons that may become clearer in the following pages, I have decided that the word "God" is good enough.

I am also a child of my culture. Older now, I have seen too much unhappiness and suffering in North America to believe that we have some manifest destiny to the world. However, I have seen enough goodness that I refuse to write off America as an evil empire. I write from my perspective, which is both in the heart of that empire and on the edge of it—in that particular colony called Canada.

For the last eleven years of my life I have been living with refugees at a place called Romero House, which is really four houses for a community serving refugees. In this context, people from many different cultures and other religions have become my friends and neighbors. With them, I have been forced to go beyond easy tolerance or mere respect for other religions. I have come to see our many faiths as so many great rivers, which are all flowing toward the same vast ocean of the mystery of God. To reach that ocean you must get your feet wet, you must dive into one of the rivers and swim. Standing on the shore, testing all the waters, looking for the one perfect river, will get you nowhere. I know that I have become a better Christian through all my years of living with Buddhists, Jews, Muslims, Hindus, and Christians from other denominations. I hope they are better swimmers in the rivers of their traditions for having lived among those of us who are called Christians. We have become ourselves for each other.

Because of this experience, I have some reason to hope that although this book is written from an explicitly Christian perspective it will still be accessible to those of other religions and indeed to any person who is seeking a more human way of life.

With my friends and neighbors I have also been introduced to the culture of poverty and the suffering of injustice. Living with them, I have shed many skins of what I had thought was spirituality. In ordinary and extraordinary ways, they have taught me a great deal about gratitude and about what makes it more difficult to be grateful. Torture has a name and a face. He lives in the room next to me and at night it sometimes becomes his chamber of horrors. The children of an African massacre reach for my hand. Mama? Ma soeur? Minha amiga? They are always by my side, the eyes of my eyes as I write.

However, although I wrote this book with them, I did not write this book for them but rather for those who, like myself, have been shaped by a somewhat educated sort of middle-class experience. Why? Because these are the people who form the backbone of the mainline religions in North America and who are at the forefront of most new developments in spirituality. They are usually overlooked, their problems minimized, their potential underestimated, in many conversations about the extremes of rich and poor in America.

All too often, middle-class people tend to think of liberation in psychological or spiritual terms or become involved in issues of justice out of guilt rather than gratitude. I hope this book will mark a path of liberation for them and I trust that they will meet others like my neighbors along the way. Those who are more theologically inclined may want to refer to the notes at the back of the book to pursue some of the questions raised in these reflections.

Chapter seven remains to be written in the lives of the readers. As on the seventh day of creation, there is always enough time and space to pause, even to pray. Throughout this book, there are prayers that provide spaces to breathe. Some may wish to begin with them, as I did; others may choose to bypass these prayers altogether. They are there, offerings not entirely my own.

————————

Create us anew O God.
Create us not novel but new.

From the remainders of our dreams
    create a new hope O God
From the ashes of our failures
    create a new spirit O God
From the castoffs of our words
    create a new song O God
From the crutches of our lives
    create a new dance O God
From the leftovers of our loves
    create a new heart O God
From the pieces of our lives
    recreate us O God.

Hover over our darkness and depths.
Create us once again
as on the first day of creation.

————————

Be
Still. My Soul
Attend. Attend.
Do not snatch and grab

Do not grab and run
Do not flip
to the next channel
of the Universe.
Attend. Attend.
To what flows
in the midst of flux
To what fires and
is not consumed
To what stays
and satisfies.

Be attentive
to the graciousness
the glory and the goodness
that is here
that is now
ever new.
Amen.

CHAPTER TWO

Perpetual Dissatisfaction

It is the ingratitude that blinds us.
Our failure to see what we have
  on the way to getting more
Our disregard for what we step over
  on the way to somewhere else
Our lack of attention to the person by our side
  on the way to someone else
Our dismissal of the good that we do
  on the way to something greater.

All that we take for granted
  falls through our hands
  and disappears from sight.
And we too fall away
  from ourselves and from You.
We walk by ourselves
  by the wayside
  and do not recognize You
  on the way to something better.

The eyes of my eyes.
I saw my own backyard, as if for the first time, during a conversation with a teenager from Africa. A refugee from a long conflict on that continent, she had arrived on our doorstep with nothing

more than an overnight bag. After I had welcomed her and shown her the bedroom that would be hers, I invited her to have a cup of tea with me in the kitchen at the back of the house. We were able to chat a little as she had picked up some English on her long journey to North America. At one point in the conversation, she put down her cup of tea and looked intently out the window.

"Who live there?"

"No one lives out there," I replied. I was pretty sure I knew what was going on in my own backyard.

"No," insisted the young girl. "Person there. House there." She pointed in the direction of the backyard. "House there. Person there."

It was then that I saw. I saw the garage as if for the first time. The words fell from my mouth like stones.

IT. IS. A. HOUSE. FOR. A. CAR.

We both took a second look at the garage, which no longer seemed so normal. The other volunteers also began to look at the house for a car every time we sat down to eat. It loomed large in our imagination and in our prayer. We began to dream and to scheme. Given the housing crisis in the city, we decided to turn the house for a car into a room for a person. Then began the long journey in search of a building permit. As we went through the bureaucratic maze at City Hall, there were countless conversations and letters, which could be summarized in this way:

"We want to turn the house for a car into a room for a person."

"You can't do that."

"Why?"

"Because."

"Because why?"

"Because then everyone would do it."

"Wouldn't that be great!"

A look of terror comes over the bureaucrat's face. "But then there would be no room for the cars." Permission denied.

A new alternative began to take shape during conversations over afternoon tea. The house for a car would be turned into a house for God, a little meditation room. Only this time there would be no attempt to get a building permit from City Hall. Now wise as serpents, we were sure there was some zoning bylaw that would prevent us from building a house for God in our backyard.

———————————

The long look at the car had become a process of clarification. What I had once accepted as a matter of course now seemed entirely questionable. Bits of conversations came together in my mind as I focused on the car that would leave its house for the highway.

A driven man is driving along a familiar highway
past the usual signs and signals.
Then one day, on a day like every other day,
he pulls over to the side of the road,
pulled up short. He wonders
where he is going, where everyone is going,
so fast and so furiously.
He bows his head on the wheel
and intones: *I would like to be happy.*

Still memories beckon back
to the time when he wondered
about the cloud in the sky which hung there
just hung there
forever
to the time when the girl of his dreams
looked at him steady and sure and said
You matter to me
to the time when he watched

his child sleeping and realized
she was better *than anything*
we could have planned.

He clenches his hands on the wheel
and again tries to get a grip on himself.

His wife sits and watches the evening news
about yet another disaster.
She flips through the channels of the universe
in a state of remote control. She flips
past the clip about the man who refused
to leave his car by the side of the road.
Maybe he lost his way.
Maybe he doesn't know where he is going.

Minutes before she had a call
from a market research man asking
for her preference in political parties,
fast food, pet projects, and cars.
Does it really matter?

The driver could be a woman, young or old, you or I who live in America, the North and the West in a time of endings and beginnings. The fact that he is driving a car suggests that he is not poor, although he may be in debt. Without a face and a name, he or she is, nonetheless, recognizable. An existence in a lane so fast that one forgets where it started and where it will all end up. An existence so driven that it becomes almost impossible to notice anyone else in the same lane or those who live by the side of the road, on the streets and in the back alleys. A life consumed.

He or she is the object of many surveys and statistics that measure almost everything except that incalculable quality of grace that pulls us up short, startles us afresh, and leaves us yearning for another way.

What Drives Us?

The car, of course, is more than a car. Beyond the simple fact of its existence, it stands as a testament to know-how and can-do, to the skills of engineering and entrepreneurial savvy. Cities are constructed around its needs and habits, houses are built in its name, nations are held together by highways, countless thousands depend on it for their livelihoods. The car is still the engine that drives our economy.

Useful in practical terms and sometimes quite necessary, the car has also become a vehicle for our identity, happiness, and meaning. When this happens, the car takes on a life of its own. We do not drive it. The car drives us.

Through advertising the car becomes more than merely useful. It symbolizes everything we could and should want. Value-added. This is not to suggest that we are all passive recipients of what the producers of advertisements feed us. We, in a sense, feed the advertising industry and together we are co-producers of a culture of values and meaning.

The car appears, whether on a television screen or in a magazine, with a certain feel to it. The fender seems to bend with a smile of assurance and the headlights seem to see ahead. Almost personal, it suggests that you could become a person, someone, if you owned it. The car becomes worth buying, even worth selling yourself for, which is what the woman next to the car is doing. Wound up like a mechanical doll, she is supposedly part of the package.

If we believe the messages that are communicated through advertising, then we will expect to *be* someone by having a car. We buy ourselves an identity. In other times and places, people identified themselves as members of a family, of a tribe, of a nation, or of a religious tradition. Now, a significant number of people identify themselves by the brand names of what they wear, what they eat, and what they drive.

Not only can the car provide us with a sense of identity, it can also promise a sense of meaning and purpose in life.

The Ultima. The Infiniti. The Maxima. The Lumina. The Aurora.

We are seduced by advertisements in which the car carries us through the deserts of life, up to the mountaintop and just to the edge. If we just drive fast enough, or so we are led to believe, we may be able to sustain the illusion that we are going somewhere.

And it promises even more. The car will make us happy. It will help us pick up an attractive stranger. The pets will have fun in it. Our families may grow closer as we drive off together. The car is the vehicle of the American dream. It lets us drive out independent and free and then drive back to its house and our home. Buick saves and sets you free.

All of these promises tap into our most profound human desires: the search for identity, the quest for meaning, and the longing for happiness. Through advertising, these spiritual desires are diverted and converted into cravings—for things, for a lifestyle rather than a life, for what is doomed to obsolescence rather than for what endures. Herein lies the secret of marketing success and the source of much of our unhappiness. For the sake of a car we will slave, we will work and overwork, we will go into debt. Even the poorest of the poor can be driven by such an illusion.

The car carries more than the passengers. It becomes so freighted with significance that we assume it needs and deserves shelter and protection. Houses for cars seem less debatable than houses for people and for God.

The problem is not the car but rather what we make of it. The car is only one obvious example of the driven and dissatisfying life that is consuming us all.

The Culture of Money

How has it come to pass that we have invested so much of ourselves in things such as cars? The answer has less to do with personal or moral weakness than with the overwhelming influence of consumerism in our lives. Its effect is all the more controlling because it is so subtle and so pervasive. The chains that hold us captive are not visible but they are, nonetheless, real. They are strengthened by countless illusions. Advertising, like all propaganda, works through repetition—anything repeated often enough becomes true.

I assume that most readers of this book are slightly wary of the more conspicuous forms of consumerism and see them as at least silly. They would probably not set their sights on luxury liners, stockpiles of shoes, or an armory of diamonds. However, I suspect that most of us remain largely unconscious of the extent to which consumerism reaches deep within us and operates as a psychological and even spiritual dynamic.

The statistics about the influence and prevalence of advertising should at least give us pause: The average American, who watches TV for twenty-six hours a week, will by the end of his or her life have watched thirteen continuous years of programming. Since advertising takes up 27 percent of prime time television, we must assume that the average American will have assimilated *three solid years of advertising alone* in the course of a lifetime. Through television and various other forms of advertisement, we are bombarded by sixteen thousand brand-name logos every day. Even those who consciously shun watching TV will find it almost impossible to escape its influence altogether, for they must live and work in a world shaped by people who have had their consciousness altered by advertising.

No one can consider these statistics and retain the innocent sense that consumerism is only about shopping.

Consumerism is the dynamic created by our very own brand of materialism, American materialism. Our made-in-the-West materialism has the potential to diminish and distort the human spirit just as much as historical materialism destroyed the desire for hope and meaning in the lives of those who lived under communism.

We could call our brand of materialism capitalism, or late industrial capitalism, or the new capitalism, but this would be to remove it somewhat from ourselves and leave it as the preserve of bankers and economists. I find it more helpful to refer to this as the culture of money—because it is a culture with its own set of values, its own spirit, symbols, and codes of communication. As a culture, it is far more influential than the culture of democracy or the culture of religion. While there are many and diverse cultures within the Western world, the one predominant culture that knows no bounds is the culture of money.

The destructiveness of materialism lies neither in material things nor in the businesses of producing them and selling them. Christianity, which is based on the belief that the Word of God became flesh, has always had a healthy respect for the material things of life—the body, sexuality, food, money, buildings and shelters. The devastation begins when material realities begin to consume us as human beings and to drive our social and political goals. Economics is a useful tool, but it is neither a wise master nor a just god.

The Captivity of Craving

Ours is a culture constituted through craving. It works as long as people want more, want to go shopping, want to think that freedom has to do with the range of choices available to the shopper. Without consumption there would be no production—and no profit.

The problem is not the shopping that is a normal part of sustaining existence. The problem arises when we think that we are buying identity, meaning, and purpose in the process. According to ancient wisdom, identity, meaning, and happiness are discovered rather than purchased. They are discovered through a long and sometimes arduous process rather than with the quick swipe of a card. And another and another and then again another.

We are held captive when our deep spiritual longings are transformed into cravings for more. Once we buy the car of our dreams, we begin to dream of another car, a bigger and faster car. To satisfy this craving we will work longer and harder or will take on a job that is unsatisfying in a daily sort of way. Or there may be a modest hope for a more family-friendly van and for the sake of this we will take work home or go into the office on the weekends. The inflation of work.

The microchip itself crystallizes this craving. We want smaller and faster technological gadgets. The laptop which once seemed like such a convenience now fails to satisfy. As we assimilate the countless visualizations of what better computers can do, we want a faster machine with all possible options. We are told, and so we believe, that this will save us time. Once again we swipe the card. Once again we wonder why we are too busy to enjoy our friends and family.

However, the craving may also take on many and various and more subtle forms. It may be a craving for more experiences: a walk on the wild side, a trip to an island in the sun or a wilderness retreat. It may be a craving for more relationships, or deeper relationships, or more sexually satisfying relationships. It may be a craving for more information, for another interesting course, for more insight and self-knowledge. It may even be a craving for more spirituality. Genuine spiritual longings can become the most sophisticated form of craving for more. Look at the thriving business in things spiritual: music, books, incense, aromas, and crystals. It is so easy to capitalize on these spiritual longings for more, for a better life, a deeper life, that certain forms of spirituality in North America reflect and even reinforce the consumer culture.

In any case, what once seemed like a luxury becomes a need and then even a basic need, so "second nature" to us that we feel like we will die without it. It is not unusual to hear people say, *I will die if I don't have it.* The shape of that "it" may vary from person to person. For one person it may be, *I will die if I can't travel.* Another may sense that *I will die if I don't have more intimate relationships.* And yet another may say, *I will die if I don't have more intense spiritual retreats.* Travel, intimacy, and spiritual retreats are all good in themselves, but when our need for them is linked to our fear of death then we are held captive by a spirit of craving.

Culturally Induced Dissatisfaction

The craving for more is inversely experienced as the sense that what we have is NEVER ENOUGH. When the billionaire Howard Hughes was once asked how much money it would take to make him happy, he reportedly replied "just a little bit more." In the culture of money, we begin to believe that if we just had a little bit more of whatever we would be happy but what we have now is not enough. The objects of our craving may change, but the dissatisfaction will remain.

Consumerism works only as long as we are even slightly dissatisfied with what we have. We cast our eyes around the things we have bought at great price, at the experiences we have accumulated and the relationships we have acquired and find them all somehow...wanting.

This dissatisfaction is not natural. It is a culturally induced dissatisfaction that is essential to the dynamic of the culture of money. It is a spirit of craving that swirls around us and within us, as pervasive as the air we breathe. It is a dissatisfaction that will never be alleviated, because if it were we would not go shopping, we would not seek out more experiences, relationships, information, or whatever, and then the whole system would collapse. We are enticed by the promise that with just a little bit more of whatever we would be happy and satisfied. Many more people are working harder and longer in order to get "just a little bit more." Some are literally working themselves to death, and yet they would not take the offer of a little more time if it meant getting a little less money. We are held captive by dissatisfaction.

Sometimes a parent sees the reality of this captivity only when she watches her children and realizes: *It used to take so little to make me happy when I was a kid. Now they are never satisfied.* Yet, she feels unable to resolve the dissatisfaction: *The less time I have to spend with them the more I feel guilty and the more I buy them gifts.*

There is a wasting in such wanting. The good things we have are tossed away as new ones are purchased. Relationships and commitments that once satisfied become more disposable. Meaning, sometimes purchased at great price, can become obsolete. It becomes easier to dispose of people in the political process, to discount those who are not big consumers. It becomes more possible to believe in economic systems that lay waste the lives of human beings and the resources of the earth. We begin to believe that we too are of little account or worth. Who we are is consumed in the process of becoming someone else.

There is a waste of everything, including time. Such wanting does not linger in the present moment. We are too busy to live, too busy to consider another way of living. If we reflect on our efforts to find more time, to make more time, we may realize how much we have been diminished in the process. Getting through, getting ahead, and getting away can become an all-consuming process. The sheer velocity of life seems to carry us forward, but we may be just running on the spot. Time itself becomes the experience of captivity. Free time becomes the stuff of memories and dreams.

The very busy feel as if they are being consumed by lack of time and those who have little to do are oppressed by the burden of too much time. Indeed, those with too much time are somehow socially suspect.

This artificially induced dissatisfaction afflicts all types and classes of people. It is manifest in the unhappiness of the rich such as Howard Hughes, in the anxious strivings of the middle class, and in the bitter resentments of the poor who sit and watch the young and the restless and the bold and the beautiful drive their cars. In this general atmosphere of dissatisfaction, it becomes more difficult to recognize those real situations in which "a little bit more" would indeed mean a measure of happiness. It is easy to dismiss the "whining" of the poor when you feel so enslaved yourself.

Such dissatisfactions are not the stuff of social revolutions because we continue to be seduced by the hope that "a little bit" more might make a real difference.

A Deeper Dissatisfaction

We get the message that it is never enough. But it doesn't stop there. It stays with us even when the shopping seems done for a while.

Slowly but surely this message transmutes and transforms us at other levels of our being:

> **I don't have enough**
> becomes **I am not enough**
> becomes **I am not good enough**

To say "I am not enough" is to acknowledge a generalized sense of powerlessness. It is all those feelings that gnaw away at the hopes we have treasured: *I can't do much about it. It won't make any difference if I try. It's just impossible. Why should I care anyway? That's the way things are. He'll never change, he's always been like that. She'll never make it. We'll never make it. They're losers. We're losers. You can't take on the whole system. Don't waste your time.*

To say "I am not good enough" is to admit a vague feeling of guilt. It is those feelings that claw us from the inside out: *Who am I to say? I've never suffered that way. I should have done more. I could have done more. I shouldn't have said that. I don't have the right to tell anyone what to do. We have to clean up our own act first. It must be my fault. It must be America's fault. It's up to us.*

In other words, the economically induced dissatisfaction in the culture of money not only drives us to shop, it also produces a profound dissatisfaction with one's very self, one's very soul, the core of one's being.

It generates within us profound feelings of powerlessness and inadequacy or guilt. Let me suggest that the intrinsic link between the dynamics of the economy, the psyche, and the spirit may go some way to explaining the curious situation in which so many North Americans, who live in the richest and most powerful nations on earth, feel generally powerless and vaguely guilty. It may help shed light on some of the rather perplexing self-hatred and self-deprecation of a good number of people in North America. It may help us reflect on why so many feel there is "not enough" to go around and so are driven to a politics of scarcity in nations of great material wealth.

The connection between the so-called "outer" world of economics and the "inner" life of the self may also offer some insight into why so many people who are relatively well off (in comparison to the vast majority of people in the world) still feel generally unhappy.

It is precisely the vagueness of the generalized feelings that flow from this all-encompassing sense of dissatisfaction which makes them so debilitating. Real feelings of powerlessness are based on realistic assessments of things in our lives or in the world, things that we cannot change. Through such an assessment we are usually left with a renewed sense of what we can change. Vague feelings of powerlessness, on the other hand, seem unrelated to any particular situation or reality and can lead to general feelings about the meaninglessness of one's life or actions: *Nothing I do or say will make a difference. My life doesn't matter.*

Similarly, real guilt as opposed to vague guilt can become the source of renewed energy—both spiritual and psychological. Real guilt locates us as human beings who have the capacity (and power) to do good or ill. To sense that we have done wrong is also to begin to reclaim our potential to do good. The person who feels really guilty is also in the process of realizing that his or her actions have consequences, that life is not inconsequential. However, one can feel overwhelmed by vague feelings of guilt. "I am not good enough." We can feel that we are responsible for much that is wrong with the world or we can feel guilty about everything that is wrong in our family—and quite unsure of whether we can do anything about it just as we are unsure about what exactly we have done to make things go wrong.

This lack of conviction about the significance of one's actions can manifest itself in at least two ways. On the one hand, a person may feel paralyzed, unable to do or to say anything. On the other, a person may engage in a frenzy of activity and be perpetually busy. Such busyness usually results from an inability to say no to anything because we are not convinced that it matters whether we say yes to something. If we aren't convinced that the choices we make matter, then we might as well do everything that comes along. Paralysis and hyperactivity are both symptoms of a sense of insignificance and powerlessness.

A Wider Dissatisfaction

The deep dissatisfaction generated by the dynamic of craving can also manifest itself in a general dissatisfaction with other people, with one's work, with the world, and with one's church or religious tradition. It is the generalized nature of this dissatisfaction that is so destructive and that makes it more difficult to identify those specific realities with which we should be dissatisfied. Although some of the symptoms of this generalized dissatisfaction may resemble depression, it is an attitude that can afflict people who seem to be able to function in their daily lives.

It is manifest in the refusal to acknowledge the measure of goodness in each person and in the judgment that the other is never "good enough." It is the tendency to want the other to be better, to be more loving, more caring, more efficient, more sensitive, more humorous, more successful, more beautiful, more together. It is the tendency to discount moments of strength as only temporary, to dismiss signs of change as aberrations, to belittle what is done or said as "not enough." It is evident when parents ask too much or the wrong things from their children and when children wish they had better parents.

There are, of course, quite specific and real reasons for real disappointment in a relationship and there are relationships that seem like nothing but disappointment. However, when every relationship seems dissatisfying, then we should ask ourselves whether a culturally induced dissatisfaction has made us consumers of relationships.

This dissatisfaction can extend even to the world in general, to the institutions that govern our lives, the companies that employ us, the projects we work on, and the communitarian efforts we are involved in. Hardly anyone can believe, of course, that the world is as it should be, that every institution is perfect, or that all human projects are right and good. We should never adjust to injustice or adapt to corruption and violence. Yet, we should take stock to determine whether we feel *only* dissatisfaction with the way things are. If we cannot find any small moments of satisfaction, cannot see anything that is better than it used to be, cannot relish one small moment of accomplishment, then our view of the world is being consumed by a general sense of dissatisfaction.

This dissatisfaction is soul-destroying and dispiriting. It makes it almost impossible to cherish the world and to embrace it with passionate care.

Similarly, if we see the church only as not good enough, not just enough, not spiritual enough, then we must wonder whether we have been afflicted in yet another way by a general sense of dissatisfaction. If we cannot find one good thing to say about our church then we have become yet another dissatisfied consumer of religion.

Finally, what are we to make of a deep and persistent dissatisfaction with God who never seems to do enough or to care enough or to be politically correct enough? To whom shall we go when even God seems not good enough?

Will we always be waiting for something more to happen in our own lives, in the lives of others, and in our world? In the meantime, it is just possible that we may be missing the goodness that is already within us and around us. A general sense of dissatisfaction consumes our time, our relationships, our work, and our very selves. We are held captive by the illusion that we could be satisfied with just a little more. Who or what will set us free?

Partial Liberations

Within most churches there is a tendency to deal with feelings of vague guilt and a generalized sense of powerlessness as personal problems that need pastoral care. We have some very well trained ministers who can and do use a wide variety of psychological approaches to heal feelings of false guilt and inadequacy or to deal with negative self-images. There are also programs of spirituality and various types of retreats whose purpose is to develop a deeper awareness of God's love so that a person can be freed from the afflictions of false guilt and a sense of personal worthlessness.

There are helpful therapies that assist people in identifying some of the roots of dissatisfaction in their own personal backgrounds. There are some remedies for perfectionism as a personal syndrome. There are wise spiritual guides who know how to distinguish between psychologically based dissatisfaction and the deeper existential dissatisfaction that is one side of the mysterious longing for God.

All of these approaches can be helpful and no one should deny the fact that many people have been genuinely aided by such pastoral approaches. However, these programs can never be completely helpful as long as the underlying dynamic in the culture of money continues unabated. If the spirit of craving continues to gnaw away at the heart and soul of our culture, even programs of healing and empowerment will leave us with the feeling that even they are NOT ENOUGH and that we need MORE.

This should at least make us consider the claim that spirituality may succeed where organized religion has failed. The resurgence of interest in spirituality is more than understandable given the extent to which it has been repressed by the enlightened world of the West. The twentieth century may have been a time of sexual liberation, but it kept the spiritual dimension of life suspect or, at least, separate. Just as religion took place on Sunday, so too spirituality was associated with certain times and places and special people.

Now spirituality has become a more widespread preoccupation, but personal liberation cannot be complete as long as the world remains untransformed. Although spirituality may provide a cloister for the self or an enclave for like-spirited people, it does so at its own peril. It may be necessary to take refuge from the wearying world for a while, but the world cannot be escaped forever. The world is within us as deep-seated dissatisfaction that will not let us go. The search for spirituality can itself become a consuming process. Churches that want to become more "seeker friendly" or who plan to "use" spirituality to bolster their flagging fortunes should reflect on the extent to which the spirit of the culture of money holds them captive.

It may also be helpful for more fundamentalist Christians to reflect on how many of the things that properly trouble them are tied to the inner dynamic of the culture of money—the consumption of values and relationships, the corrosion of character, the disappearance of loyalties and commitments. Religion alone cannot establish solid values and relationships as long as the culture of money remains unquestioned and untransformed.

There are, of course, those who attempt to address the social and economic causes of what appear to be personal problems. It is their analysis that the present economic system is the root of all evil and that any social or personal transformation must begin with or, at least, include economic change. There are people, religiously committed people and men and women of good will, who hunger and thirst for justice. However, if this hunger for justice is more akin to a craving for a *more* just and perfect world, then even the finest efforts for justice will replicate the patterns of craving that lie close to the heart of our culture. If the work for justice is driven by a general dissatisfaction with the world, with other people, and with institutions, then it will never lead to profound or lasting social change.

Social critique is essential, but it can become a generalized judgment that nothing or no one, including oneself, is good enough. Such social dissatisfaction eventually consumes even those working for justice. It is crucial, in my experience, that every effort for justice include some process for differentiating a general dissatisfaction with the world from a real hunger and thirst for justice—which Jesus promised would be satisfied, at least a little, here and now. Genuine social and political change can happen only if it is based on or accompanied by an attempt to transform the spirit of craving and dissatisfaction. Otherwise, this spirit can consume even the attempts to construct an alternative to it. Such radical transformation is risky because the spirit of craving can consume even its enemies and critics. We may, for example, attempt to stifle the spirit of craving by living a simpler lifestyle only to find ourselves consumed with the thought that we are never living simply enough. Even those who set out to fight the spirit of craving can tend to replicate its patterns of vague guilt and powerlessness within themselves.

Similarly, if we attempt to involve people in the process of changing the world by tapping into their vague feelings of guilt, then we will end up by undercutting their capacity to do some specific good in the world. If we try to engage people in a just cause by encouraging them to identify with the powerless of the world, then they will do nothing more than project their own sense of powerlessness onto others, leaving them only with a vague dissatisfaction with their lives, without any conviction that what they do matters.

Liberation from the spirit of craving will not come easily or quickly. It has become so all encompassing and all consuming that a program of personal liberation or a new political or economic agenda to make things better will not suffice. Liberation from our North American activity will surely involve all of this as necessary but not sufficient. Because we are held captive at the deepest level of our being, the liberation must at least begin there and be sustained from there.

How can we be set free? Can we liberate ourselves from this dispiriting dissatisfaction? Can we hope for anything beyond being dissatisfied with our dissatisfaction?

Captivity Then and Now

Enmeshed as we are in the culture of money, we find it difficult to see our way through. We have become so accustomed to
our subtle form of captivity that it seems almost normal and it is
difficult to imagine an alternative way of being. It is helpful, therefore, to review the religious responses forged in other situations of
captivity in order to discover some insight into our own situation.
Captivity is as old as it is new.

In reviewing the experiences of captivity as they are recorded
in the bible, I have found that the revelations associated with the
experience of the Babylonian captivity have much to say to us
today. In referring to this particular captivity, the time when the
Jewish people were expelled from their land and taken to the
Babylonian empire, I am consciously choosing a paradigm that, I
think, is most appropriate to the North American context.

Within the biblical tradition, the experience of the Babylonian
captivity was crucial in the formation of the Jewish people's sense
of identity, meaning, and purpose. It was during the time of captivity that they came to a new understanding of their God as the
One Who Creates and a renewed understanding of the world, the
material world, as God's creation.

It was during the time of captivity that prophets were called
forth to tell the people why they were in captivity. Prophets
such as Jeremiah and Ezekiel did not tell the people that they
were innocent and helpless victims of some ruthless superpower.
These prophets spoke the unpopular message that the people
were in captivity because of choices they had made, because
they had worshipped what they had produced and manufactured, things made of money, of silver and gold. "They worshipped worthless idols and have become worthless themselves"
(Jer 2:4). It is said that the people were even willing to sacrifice
their own offspring for consumption, offering them to Moloch,
the god who ate children.

For those who had ears to hear, the message of the prophets was devastatingly clear: The people had been led into captivity long before the invasion of the Babylonians because their religious and political leaders had been captivated by the illusion that they could buy and sell identity, meaning, and happiness. The problem was not that the people engaged in economic activity, in the business of making a living. The problem was that they began to worship it, and submitted their whole lives to its demands.

Interestingly enough, it was not the poor who were taken away from Israel into captivity in Babylon. The poor were allowed to stay in their own land because they posed no threat and were of no account to the new Babylonian masters. It was the elites, the religious and intellectual elites and the skilled workers, who were forced to go to the Babylonian empire—where they could be controlled and used.

For a while the elites sat by the rivers of Babylon and wept about their situation. But eventually, over several generations, they adjusted and even thrived in Babylon, the nation of businessmen (Ez 16:28). The situation of captivity became almost normal as their memories of their own land and their own faith dimmed. The elites had become part of the system of empire and the leaders of the captive people dined regularly with the Babylonian rulers.

At times, some of the people lamented the fact that they had no effective leadership, that all of their political and religious institutions had collapsed and with them the structures of meaning that had sustained their identity and faith. They were left with only the fragments of former rituals and the shards of their tradition.

It was then that a prophet called Second Isaiah was summoned forth to draw the people away from the illusions of happiness that had supplanted the dream of the reign of God. Drawing on all his evocative power as a poet, he recalled the vision of another way of being. Appealing to memory rather than nostalgia, he provided a real basis for hope: "The spirit of the Lord is upon me for God has anointed me. He has sent me to bring good news to the afflicted, to soothe the broken-hearted, to proclaim liberty to captives" (Is 61:1).

However difficult this experience of captivity, it was, nevertheless, an important religious moment in the history of the Jewish people. It was then that they began to reflect on how their God was different from the god of empire, the god of an ancient culture of money. They understood that the god who controlled and destroyed could never be the One Who Creates.

Poets and thinkers began to ponder an alternative view of life and wrote down their own story of the way the world is and was in the beginning of time and history. It was during this experience of exile and captivity that the Jewish people put to song and verse their own creation story, which endures today as the book of Genesis.

This story of creation begins with the remarkable words "In the beginning." It is the story of a world created out of nothing but love. It is the story of a world created for nothing but love. In the beginning was a single moment of pure grace, a moment which human beings could neither plan nor produce but which could, nonetheless, be recognized with amazement.

This brief and very selective reading of the exilic texts offers some insight into our own North American context where we are in captivity, within a global empire, but now the king has no name or face or perhaps many names and faces.

We are in captivity because we have made a god out of an economic system and have worshipped it as if it were the only reality.

Most of us use much more prosaic language in our incantations of our contemporary idols. We refer to "the economy" as "reality" and we adjust continually to its requirements, accepting poverty and unemployment as normal. We chant the praises of "the bottom line" and "corporate restructuring." We believe it is the prerogative of "the economy" to bestow the blessings and punishments of wealth and poverty and to determine that these are, indeed, blessings and punishments. Our lives go up and down as the markets rise and fall.

We are sacrificing our young people to this idol. We tell them that "getting a job" is far more important than finding their calling in life. We are willing to let them become slaves and functionaries of a system, willing to tell them that a good salary more than compensates for lack of happiness. We are willing to turn our educational systems into a business for businesses.

Too many who deal in the business of knowledge and religion seem strangely unable to question the underlying cultural assumptions that hold us captive. In a few cases, this inability may be linked to their ease in dining at the tables of businessmen or to the comforts of the professional academic or church world. However, I suspect that many members of our intellectual and religious elites see and do not see simply because they are not convinced that what they do or say will make any difference.

It is all too easy to lament the lack of leadership in these times. However, the idols are not out there and the worshippers are not other than ourselves. They are within each of us, in our unconscious assumptions of what reality is and can be.

It can be difficult to live in a time and place of captivity such as North America, but it need not be destructive. A time of captivity *if it is recognized as such* can also be a time of liberation. Like the people of Israel in captivity, we have a choice as to how we deal with our situation: we can adjust to the culture in which we find ourselves or we can recognize our very real captivity and weep by the rivers of memory. The potential for religious renewal can be discovered through such a recognition. As the people in captivity in Babylon discovered that their God was essentially a God of creative power, so we too are invited to reflect on how God is different from the gods of the culture of money. We too can look on the world as something very good, as something grand and given. We too can be moved to awe, to astonishment, and to gratitude.

Such an awareness can make all the difference in the world. It will affect the quality of our relationships, with whom we spend our time, whether our work is life giving or death dealing, when we can sleep easy and how we get up in the morning...and why.

We cry out to You because
living is so all-consuming
we are wasting away
from wanting it all.
We are too busy
to take the one step.
We are running in circles
running on the spot
getting ahead
while falling behind
going nowhere fast.
Thus we are held captive
to everything and nothing.

Let us take the one step
the one sure step
in the direction of freedom.
One step is enough.
Let us go. Let us leave
Mardok, Mammon,
the disposable gods.
Be with us Manna,
Daily Bread and ordinary delight.
Give us water on the way,
You, the Diviner. You, the Destination.

———————

You have saved me.
Nothing has been thrown away.
When I lost my smile
You planted it again as flowers.

When the music stopped
  You set it in a sea shell.
When hope blew away
  You caught it in a sail.
When my tears fell You sent them back
  again as snowflakes onto my cheeks.
When friends took flight
  You held them in a nesting place.
When I walked away
  You held me in Your heart.

You have not thrown anything away
You have not thrown me away
You have saved me in Yourself.

Chapter Three

Radical Gratitude

We walk on the waters of gratitude
knowing there is nothing there
trusting there will be enough
to go on.
We were drowning in the boat
consumed by the work
of getting ahead, getting around
getting to it all.

Now we walk on held up
by nothing but memories
of how love becomes solid
when it is given away
of how loaves multiply
when shared among many
of how we become sure
and serene on the water.

There is a moment each day when it is morning before it is morning. Darkness still hovers over the deep. Those who wait for the dawn can hear it even before they see it. At first there are only the slight sounds of attunement as a chorus of birds assembles: twits and trills, chirps and peeps, and even the occasional squawk.

Slowly they gather into one great concerted song of supplication: Let it begin! Let us begin! May it begin again!

They are of one accord. They do not take the dawn for granted. When it bursts upon them, once again, as on the first day of creation, they give thanks once again for this once only day, to begin.

The birds know, as we sometimes do, that the light does not dawn because of our singing. We sing because the dawn appears as grace.

———————

How we begin a day affects how we will live that day. Many of us begin the day in a rather mechanical way—jarred into motion by the ring of an alarm clock or the sound of coffee dripping. We have set the time to begin, or so we believe, and thus we take the possibility of each new day for granted. All the gadgets of technology leave us with the illusion that we are, or should be, in control of how our day begins, proceeds, and ends. Automatically we move, in the presumption of life.

In this culture, it is not easy to awaken to the marvelous gift of each day and to recognize that it is not necessarily so. We tend to take this ordinary beginning for granted, just as we take ourselves, and others, and the world—life itself—for granted.

Whatever and whoever we take for granted can easily become just another thing in our lives, something else to be worked on, managed, or consumed. We become oblivious. The realities we take for granted can no longer be recognized as an amazing grace, can rarely astonish us into life, will never set us free.

Our general dissatisfaction with ourselves, with others, and with the world is possible only as taking for granted becomes a habit of being. We can want more because we assume we already have something or someone.

For example: I can want air conditioning only because I can presume there is air to breathe. I can want tastier meals only because I already have some food. I can want a better life for my children only when I can assume their very existence is not in doubt. I can hope to be healthier and more whole only when I can take the fact that I am alive for granted.

What we overlook begins to waste away. Will clean air and food come to us as a matter of course if we take the earth for granted? Can any relationships endure if they are merely taken for granted? What happens when we can neither take ourselves too seriously nor too lightly but only for granted?

In the culture of money, we tend to have a ledger view of life. We add up the pluses and minuses and try to account for our lives. In the process, we miss the amazing fact that we even have a life to add up. We take being alive for granted and move on to a cost-benefit analysis. Lost in the process is the incalculable mystery of simply being alive. The liberation of gratitude begins when we stop taking life for granted.

We will be liberated from the captivity of craving for more only by an attitude of radical gratitude. To begin to understand this attitude we must throw away the ledgers of our lives. This attitude is much more than the occasional thank you note and cannot be confined to a spirituality in which the self is cloistered from the harsh realities of the world. Radical gratitude is not only spiritual, but because it is also spiritual in the widest and deepest sense, it carries with it the promise of spiritual, psychological, political, and economic liberation. I cannot prove that such is the case but I can give some account of why I believe it may be so.

Radical gratitude is as real as it is mysterious. As a revelation, it may come as momentous, earth shattering and sky opening. However, more often than not it appears in a deft sort of way. Then, if we will, we become witnesses, telling stories of grace.

Here follows my testament and the stories of others who bear witness to radical gratitude.

Stories of Gratitude

My Beginning

A few years ago, I was shocked into wonder at the miracle of my own beginning as I began to read my dad's old diary from the Second World War. It had been a closed book, or so it seemed. We knew it was up there in the attic, somewhere in Dad's old trunk. Then came the time of remembering.

As I read between the lines of his diary, I realized that I had been conceived in London, England, on V.E. Day. My mother, a young nursing supervisor, and my father, a surgeon, had been married in Canada just before the war in Europe had begun. Together they decided to go across the ocean to share their medical skills to help the wounded. They were separated for years by the English channel, my mother nursing in the south of England and then in London and my father operating in a M.A.S.H.-like unit in France, Holland, and Belgium.

Toward the end of the war, although he didn't know the end was near at the time, my father received a four-day leave for the first time since the allied invasion of France. He grabbed a motorcycle and raced across the roads of Belgium and Holland until he reached the port of Ostend on the southern coast of the channel. He could hear the boat honking its departure as he roared up the pier on his motorcycle. This was the last ferry leaving for England that night and my father caught it just in time. As darkness fell, the boat crossed the channel and he awoke to see the white cliffs of Dover. He boarded the train to London and as it pulled into Victoria Station he could hear the church bells pealing. When he walked out onto the platform, strangers ran to hug him crying, "The war is over! It's over."

In the midst of this pandemonium, he found my mother and they were able to spend the day together. My father left London the next morning and would not see my mother until a year after the war was over. Nine months after V.E. Day I was born.

All of this was recorded in my father's diary in his usual scratches and squiggles. I was, at first, surprised to learn that I had been conceived on V.E. Day in London. And then I was shocked into wonder: What if he had missed that last ferry? He would still have made it to London and had some time with my mother and probably someone would have been born nine months later but not me. For me, at least, this was a matter of crucial importance.

I was radically amazed. I realized that there was all the difference in the world between being or not being at all. I could no longer take my life for granted.

Beginning Again, Out of the Great Blue

To understand this story about beginning again, you need to know that I tend to imagine the Holy Spirit as a Great Blue Heron. This image took shape within me a few years ago when I discovered the nesting place of a heron colony over the hill behind a small cottage that we have in the country north of the city. The twenty nests topped old dead trees, which stood in the middle of a still pond completely encircled by the arms of the stone ridges. Off the beaten path and accessible only on foot, the heronry was a secret place inhabited by creatures who seemed to fly in an ancient world. In the morning mist as everything emerged from the gray, the blue herons seemed like something out of the earth's first dawn. As one took flight, the wings a-thunk a-thunk, I thought I had seen the Holy Spirit.

Of course I know the Holy Spirit is not a bird and that any of our imaginings of this Great Spirit are merely approximations. Nevertheless, I felt that the Great Blue was a truer image than the pretty white dove, which is depicted on Christmas cards, stained glass windows, and peace posters. My fascination with the great blue heron was well known by my friends and students.

And so it came to pass that one Saturday afternoon I was driving to an apartment-mall complex to visit one of the refugee families who had lived with us. As I inched into a left turn toward the entranceway, my car was hit directly on the driver's side by a fire truck, which was racing down the wrong side of the road against a red light. A mass of red and chrome passed over me.

I should have been decapitated or left with a head beyond repair, but my car was so old that my seat collapsed backwards and flattened upon impact. I was left encapsulated by the roof and the floorboard of the car. Voices started yelling, asking me if I could hear, telling me not to move. Everything felt fine to me so I just slipped sideways to the right and came out of the metal tomb. After the firemen recovered from the shock of seeing me stand up, they bundled me onto a stretcher and into an ambulance.

I was not alone. Later I would learn that a young woman with a small child in a stroller had witnessed this accident. While I was being lifted into the ambulance, she asked the attendants where they were taking me. She gathered up her child and took the next streetcar, which followed the ambulance down the road to the hospital. The young woman bought some flowers and a card and sat in the waiting room with her child until some of my friends arrived. She talked to them and said, *"I just didn't want her to be alone. I thought: What if nobody knows her? What if she's new to the city? What if she is someone's mother?"* My friends assured her that I would get her flowers and note and they asked for her phone number. Then she left. Later my friends would describe her as young and obviously quite poor.

The get well soon note was signed…from Christine Heron. Yes, that was the name on the *Thinking of You* card. The next day I phoned the number she had given only to hear "the number you have dialed is no longer in service." I went to the apartment buildings in the neighborhood and asked for her. I checked the phone book, but to no avail. I wanted so much to say thank you to this stranger who had taken me so to heart.

In one moment I knew that I had been granted a new begin-

ning, that God was with me, and that there was a point to my
being.

Christopher

I learned once again to let go of my ledger book view of life
after the birth of a little boy called Christopher. He had been long
awaited. His two parents, my friends, had already been through
the sorrow of several miscarriages. Finally, it seemed as if this
pregnancy would come to full term. We waited in hope. The child
was born and was named Christopher, the Christ-bearer. Very
soon we learned that he had a congenital defect and that his lungs
would not be able to grow along with the rest of his body. He was
weak and could not see or hear very well. His life, the doctors told
us, would be limited to a few months.

My first reaction was one of profound sorrow for my friends.
Yet, it was they who drew me beyond this sorrow and into a sense
of gratitude. Day after day, as they held his hand through the
opening in the incubator, as they sang to him through the plastic
walls surrounding his life, I could see that their hearts were more
filled with love than with sorrow. While I had been focusing on his
impending death, they were dwelling in a sense of gratitude for his
life, for the miracle of his beginning. While I was angry at what
was being taken away, they were reverencing what had been given.
For them, Christopher was more an amazing grace than a possession they had a right to hold onto.

Overwhelming Goodness on September 11

Brian Halloran came to Romero House to give a year of his
life in the service of resettling refugees. He didn't consider himself
a church-going type and he downplayed any religious reasons for
choosing to volunteer. He came from Minnesota and he looked it.
Some even speculated that he slept in his baseball cap. He was an
excellent soccer player, a better pool shark, and an even better

human being. After his time with us, he went to work in state politics. I had lunch with him in Minneapolis in the spring of 2001 and I asked him what had stayed with him after his time with the refugees. "My friendship with the Amadins," he said simply.

Muna, Assan, Mustapha, and Awad had moved into the house where Brian was the live-in coordinator. They were the same age and, like Brian, they had gone to university. However, their studies in Eritrea had been interrupted by the internal political struggles of that country. They escaped from the country in a covered truck, which took them through the desert.

Brian began to hang out with his four new Muslim friends. He admired their courage, intelligence, and pleasant attitude. "They are real quality people and they aren't afraid to be affectionate with each other." They were on welfare when they first arrived and Brian didn't earn any more than they did during his year at Romero House.

Brian returned to Minneapolis and, in the summer of 2001, he moved with his girlfriend to Manhattan. He wrote to us after September 11.

"Yes, Kirsten and I are so thankful to be alive. God took care of us the morning of September 11. I was in our apartment (three blocks east of the World Trade Center) and Kirsten was at the office (on the twentieth floor of the Woolworth building, three blocks diagonally from the World Trade Center) when the homicides occurred. After the second plane struck the second tower, we each ran toward the other person. Upon entering the area near Kirsten's building, where hundreds were streaming away from the area, I locked eyes with a tall, skinny man Kirsten had introduced me to in the subway train the night before—probably one of the only people in the city I would have recognized anyway. He told me that Kirsten was all right and they had all been evacuated from the building. I ran back to our apartment, we hugged, and began our journey away from the catastrophe. It's a good thing we found each other so quickly. We were probably ten long blocks away from the World Trade Center when the first tower collapsed, sending debris for blocks and blocks around its perimeter. Ultimately we made it to Brooklyn where a kind Puerto Rican woman we'd never met, recently off three years of welfare, took us in for the evening and assured us that 'God is watching over you.'

"I would like to speak with you, to tell you in more detail of the overwhelming goodness we've seen in the face of evil."

"Dear Brian," I thought, "so you have been saved and there is a reason for this. Now you know how precious your life is. Never squander it. Years ago you took in the Amadins who were running for their lives. So now you understand something about the great economy of grace."

The day after the bombing, Mustapha e-mailed Brian—desperately hoping that his friend had survived the attack.

A Preference for Being

I learned about radical gratitude from another young woman whom I met only as she was being interviewed on TV. Obviously afflicted by cerebral palsy, she was shaking and struggling to communicate. Nevertheless, it was possible to understand her and impossible not to be challenged by what she had to say.

"I had been burned badly," she said, "the day my bed caught fire. I was taken to the hospital and bandaged from head to toe. As I lay there, some doctors and nurses were discussing my situation. 'It might have been better if she hadn't been born,' someone remarked. As if I weren't even there.

"I thought to myself, 'Better not to have been born!' Don't they realize it's worth it? Don't they realize that it is worth being born if only to have had this one day, this one experience of lying in this bed with clean sheets?"

The Sun and Poverty

At the end of the Second World War, when Europe had been wasted away by war, a young man called Albert Camus returned from France to his native Algeria. "In the light cast by the flames," he wrote, "the world had suddenly shown its wrinkles and afflictions, old and new. It had suddenly grown old, and we had too." Spiritually and morally exhausted, he returned to his village by the Mediterranean—Tipasa, as beautiful as it was poor. "Poverty taught me that all was not well under the sun," he wrote, "but the sun taught me that poverty was not everything."

There he found new energy in the daily miracle of creation. "It was as if the morning stood still, as if the sun had stopped for an immeasurable moment. In this light and silence, years of night and fury slowly melted away." He could begin again. For Camus, this beginning again is closely linked to one's capacity for admiration, to appreciate what you have not made but which is, nonetheless, given.

For years, Camus had fought against injustice because he could not deny the reality of suffering and poverty in the world. Yet, he also refused to deny the daily miracle of creation, the shimmering light on the ocean waves and the dance of the heliotropes in the sun. Unlike his contemporary, the world-weary philosopher Jean-Paul Sartre, he begins in being rather than in nothingness.

Room Enough for Gratitude

The diaries of Etty Hillesum (published as *An Interrupted Life*) are some of the most compelling spiritual writings of this century. Written from 1941 to 1943 in Holland during the time when the Jews were being rounded up for deportation, they reveal the possibility of radical gratitude even in the darkest of times.

Etty describes herself as a sophisticated, although somewhat silly, young woman who lives in a communal household in Amsterdam. She has been studying psychology and literature, and she has taken her many lovers and a handwriting analyst terribly seriously.

Suddenly, unaccountably, she begins to feel the need to kneel in the middle of her bedroom. Feelings of overwhelming gratitude force her to her knees.

This sense of gratitude is not protected by an enclosure around her life. Etty sees her fellow Jews being rounded up in the streets and being placed on the trains to the east. She knows the fate that awaits her and yet she still notices the jasmine plant and the sky outside her window.

How exotic the jasmine looks, so delicate and dazzling against the mud-brown walls.

I can't take in how beautiful this jasmine is. But there is no need to. It is simply enough to believe in miracles in the twentieth century. And I do, even though the lice will be eating me up in Poland before long...

I often see visions of poisonous green smoke; I am with the hungry, with the ill-treated and the dying, every day, but I am also with the jasmine and with that piece of sky beyond my window; there is room for everything in a single life.

Even at a time when murder was in a state of mass production, when evil seemed most free, Etty Hillesum refused to take the beauty of the jasmine plant for granted.

Someone to Thank

I had known the outline of the story of Dorothy Day, the foundress of the radical Catholic Worker movement, for some time. However, although I knew the course of the events of her life, I couldn't quite make inner sense of it.

I knew the published facts: A radical activist with little or no interest in religion, she had been arrested for her solidarity with the poor. Escaping to Long Island for a while, she met a man called Forster who, while embracing the world of nature, had rejected God. Together they conceived a child, much to Dorothy's surprise and delight. Because of a previous abortion, she had thought she was incapable of bearing children.

Once their daughter was born, Dorothy insisted on having her baptized and began going to church. Forster left and Dorothy became a Catholic, returning to New York City where she began a house of hospitality, the first of the Catholic Worker houses. Later, Catholic workers would wonder why she would go to Mass every day even as she protested against injustices in society and wrote about the weaknesses of the church.

But why, I wondered, was the birth of the daughter the cause of both the separation from her partner and her new commitment to the church?

The pieces of her story came together for me when I read a more detailed description of the time of her daughter's birth. She was so overwhelmed with gratitude that she needed to find a way to express it. "To whom should I give thanks for so much joy?" Astonished by life, she discovered gratitude as the heart of faith and the Eucharist as its expression.

The Multiplication of Money

Several years ago, I was part of a committee that was planning a series on "prayer" at Regis College, the place where I teach theology. I suggested that we could invite Joy Kogawa, a Japanese Canadian poet and writer, to speak about "Prayer and Poetry." Joy accepted the invitation to speak and we agreed to have supper before her lecture.

In the middle of the meal, she told me: "I really have nothing to say." I know many speakers who sometimes think that, including myself. I reassured her but wondered what she really would say.

Joy was true to her word. She began her lecture by saying, "I really have nothing to say about prayer and poetry." I began to worry about all the money people had paid to come and hear her speak.

"But let me tell you what really interests me these days," she continued. I breathed a sigh of relief.

"I really want to support an aboriginal earth festival because I think we Japanese Canadians are now in a position to help other groups. However, I'm not very good at fundraising so I decided to go to the bank and take out three hundred dollars. I'm going to give each of you ten dollars and I want you to go and give ten dollars to another person and ask them to buy a ticket and give ten dollars to another person."

Then Joy walked down the main aisle of the lecture theater and began to hand out ten dollar bills to the people sitting in the audience. Then she left. People sat in silence as they looked at the money she had given them. Slowly, they too left the hall.

The next day I went into the college and someone spoke excitedly about what had happened the night before. "Did you hear about the woman who handed out hundred dollar bills?" By the end of the day, the word was going around about the woman who had handed out thousands of dollars. By the end of the week, the story had grown to epic proportions—about the lady who had handed out a million dollars.

Needless to say, the Earth Festival was well attended and well funded—even without the help of a professional fund-raiser! I was left with a precious insight into how the story of the miracle of the multiplication of the loaves and fishes might have originated and grown in the telling.

The Dynamics of Gratitude

These stories of gratitude reveal something about the inner dynamic of this attitude to life. They are not the only stories that could be told, they may not even be the best ones to tell, but they are the ones that come to the mind of my heart. They are also true stories.

I could also have told true stories of greed and self-interest, virtual or taken-for-granted lives. Our lives are directed by the stories we choose to dwell on and in.

Without defining gratitude, these stories describe the awareness that life cannot be taken for granted, that it isn't necessarily so. We are seized with amazement at what we could never have imagined, could never have manufactured on our own or managed to do.

I realized that I could not have given birth to myself. My parents surely had something to do with it. Yet the meeting of a specific egg and sperm seemed nothing short of miraculous every time I thought of that ferry leaving the pier. With each new child, someone entirely new comes into the world, and with this new person a whole new world comes into being. Dorothy Day realized this, the mystery of the creation of each person, as miraculous as the creation of the world. It is why we say that each person is a child of God.

For Brian Halloran, the unexpected arrival of help from a stranger, an assistance that was neither merited nor paid for, seemed astonishing.

Albert Camus and Etty Hillesum were sustained by the givenness of a beauty that was more than they had arranged for, that surprised them by its sudden appearance. One can see and know and understand everything about the world and still be surprised by the fact that it is there.

These stories also reveal that gratitude is possible even in the midst of great difficulty and suffering. The parents of Christopher, the woman who had been burned, and Etty Hillesum did not deny the death, which stalked them. Yet, through their acts of gratitude, they did not let themselves be defined by death and destruction. Gratitude made room for the sun in Albert Camus's life and for the jasmine in the midst of the Holocaust. Because of gratitude, death did not have dominion.

Throughout these stories there is the almost natural desire to say thank you somehow, to someone. In the awareness of having received something for free, there is a movement to wanting to acknowledge the giver. I wanted to thank Christine Heron and God as did Dorothy Day. The desire to give thanks does not come out of some compulsive guilt, but rather out of a full heart because one wants to and is happy to do so. Albert Camus and Etty Hillesum wrote in admiration and in doing so shared their sense of gratitude with others.

Joy Kogawa's action illustrates the inner dynamic of the great economy of grace: as lives and money are shared and given away there is a multiplication of resources. She bears witness to the truth of the story of the multiplication of the loaves and fishes: we can base our economy on a politics of scarcity or on a politics of abundance.

These stories of gratitude are situated within the context of very particular lives. Yet, they mean more than even what the storytellers may know to be true. They lead us to consider how the fundamental dynamic of gratitude might be particularly liberating in a culture of perpetual dissatisfaction.

Beyond Dissatisfaction

As I review my own experience and retell the stories of others, I am struck by how gratitude involves some radical satisfaction with life, with oneself, and with the world. By this I mean something qualitatively different from smug self-satisfaction or cultural contentment. I mean the awareness that one has already been given the most fundamental necessity, the gift of life. When we stop taking this first gift for granted then we can begin to experience the radical liberation of gratitude.

- Rather than wasting away from a fundamental sense of dissatisfaction with oneself, a person can begin to realize that the life he or she has been given is *enough* to begin with, *enough* to go on.

- Instead of being consumed with a sense that we should always be more—more caring, more successful, more loving, more talented—we can be sustained by the awareness that the gift of life is *enough*.

- As we set some limits on the spirit of craving and dissatisfaction which holds us captive there is an almost simultaneous liberation of a new sense of power.

- To say *I am enough* is to say that, just as I am, with all my strengths and weaknesses, I can make a difference. This is the beginning of a new sense of power.

- This is also to say *I am good enough*, which is the beginning of liberation from the vague guilt that paralyzes us in the culture of dissatisfaction.

- This awareness begins to transform us at other levels of our lives and we can begin to say *I have enough* with a happy and free spirit.

In other words, when we stop taking life for granted and recognize it as a gift that is *enough*, we are transformed at a deeply spiritual level of our lives. This transformation begins to touch other levels of our lives—to the point where we start to feel a new sense of power, a renewed hope that we can be liberated from the chains that bind us.

Slowly but surely the cultural chains that hold us captive will begin to drop. The cycle in which each promise of happiness is accompanied by an even deeper dissatisfaction will be broken. Gratitude for the gift of life takes shape as a new sense of identity, power, and purpose. *I do not have to be different or better than I am to find a measure of happiness and to be able to make a difference in the world.*

This is something quite different from mere assertiveness. It is a conviction born of gratitude that has the power to transform vague feelings of powerlessness and guilt.

I have met gifted writers who have never published a book simply because they never thought it was good enough. And what a loss this has been for all us sparrows who delight in any crumb of wisdom and beauty. Yet, I have known other writers who may not have had the same natural talent and yet were seized with the conviction that they had something to say and that the world they inhabited was significant enough to write about. Out of that conviction and energy they wrote book after book.

I have spoken with parents who had little joy in raising their children because they were always preoccupied with the thought that they should be doing something more or something different and better for their children. Yet I also have friends who started to enjoy their children once they could look at them and themselves and say with a wink, "Well, kid, I'm the only Mom you've got. It's better than nothing."

Then too, I have witnessed the liberation of children now older who have been given some sense of radical gratitude about their parents. Painfully aware of the imperfections of their parents, sometimes scarred for life by what their parents have done or not done, they may still come to this fundamental liberating awareness: *Nevertheless, were it not for them, I would not be alive.*

Countless psychological theories and social critiques acknowledge and address everything that can go wrong once one enters the world. Yet, it is that entrance, that one beginning, which is astonishing and which we so easily take for granted.

The Jewish people have a wonderful prayer of gratitude which they sing every Passover. In this song they recount the events through which God liberated them from Egypt and led them to the Promised Land. The refrain of this song is, in Hebrew, *Dayenu*, which can be translated as *It would have been enough.*

- If you had only led us to the edge of the Red Sea but not taken us through the waters, *it would have been enough.*

- If you had only taken us through the Red Sea but not led us through the desert, *it would have been enough.*

- If you had only led us through the desert but not taken us to Sinai, *it would have been enough.*

And so on. At any verse in the song, at any point in the history of liberation, it would have been enough to sing and praise God's name forever.

It is a helpful spiritual exercise to review one's own life and stop at any point with the grateful prayer *it would have been enough*. For example: If I had only been born but not had a baby sister, *it would have been enough*. If I had only had a baby sister but not had my first friend, *it would have been enough*. If I had only seen one snowfall but never seen the pink sky on a prairie night, *it would have been enough*. And so on.

In the history of Western thought there are two fundamental points of departure for reflecting on the human condition: the mystery of death and the mystery of birth. Those reflections, which take their point of departure from the keen awareness of mortality and the limitations of the human condition, can be used to highlight all the reasons we have to be dissatisfied with life. For religious thinkers, however, these considerations lead to an awareness of what is eternal in contrast to what is passing and to an acknowledgment of God as the only reality that can satisfy the longings of the human heart. There is a deep wisdom in such considerations.

It goes without saying that the dying do not tend to take life for granted. Yet, for reasons that should be obvious by now, I am suggesting that the debilitating dissatisfactions of North American culture require some reconsideration of the mystery of the human condition of natality or birth. When beginnings strike us as grace, as realities we can never take for granted, then we may begin to acknowledge the mystery of God as the creator of the universe and of each particular life. And what an astonishing difference this makes.

The Great Economy of Grace

To dwell in the mystery of beginnings is to enter into a new imagination of the world in which the most important things cannot be taken for granted yet are free. It is to enter into the great economy of grace, an economy with its own laws of production and distribution, supply and demand.

When we no longer take the world or ourselves or anyone else for granted, we begin to realize that these are things we could never have planned, organized, or manufactured. We have neither earned them nor produced them. They are free gifts from God. In the realization of such graciousness we may recognize the simple dynamic of God's love: because God loves us, we are; and, as we are, God loves us. As in the beginning of the world, so too in the beginning of each person God looks on us and sees that we are very good. This is hard for us to believe.

In the culture of money, we are held captive by the assumption that all relationships are contractual relationships in which "you can't get something for nothing." This makes it more difficult to imagine why anyone, why even God, would love us for nothing, for no reason. In our culturally adjusted forms of religion, we think there must be a reason that justifies such love: because we work hard, because we are good looking, because we are responsible, because we are religious or spiritual, because we are successful or have what really counts.

Yet, experience should teach us that we cannot earn or buy the most important things in life. We cannot manufacture love and friendship, we cannot buy affection. Relationships appear in our lives when we have stopped trying to make them happen. If we can give entirely reasonable explanations for why we love someone, then it is probably not love at all. So too, we cannot create hope. We may receive faith as a grace, act on it and strengthen it, but we cannot make ourselves believe. No amount of positive thinking, no trendy technique can produce an antidote to doubt or despair. Hope is conceived in us and we are not the parents of our own faith.

In a culture of perpetual dissatisfaction we wonder how anyone could look on us as we are and see that we are good. Surely we are never good enough, we who must always be on the way to becoming someone else.

In a consumer culture, it is not easy to believe in more enduring forms of love. It is almost beyond our imagining that God could love us not only for free but also forever. Such are the fundamental spiritual distortions of the culture of money.

The mystery of the economy of grace is that the quality of God's love is enduring and free. It breaks through any of our attempts to quantify or contain it. That which is forever and for free is also for all. The economics of God's love is not based on a law of scarcity but rather rooted in the mystery of superabundance. The personal or political decision to declare that *there is not enough* is the beginning of social cruelty, war, and violence on a petty or vast scale. On the other hand, the choice to affirm that *there is enough for all* is the beginning of social community, peace, and justice. The option to assume that *there is enough* frees the imagination to think of new political and economic possibilities.

It is only within the little weigh-scales of our mind that we think God loves some more by loving others less. Each person is loved infinitely and uniquely into being. The inherent equality in such an economics of love cannot be reduced to sameness. God's love is not simply spread out in a homogenous sort of way, but rather takes a particular and incalculable form with each person.

In the great economy of grace there is more than enough love for everyone. This includes the rich and the poor and the middle class, the ones who are near and the ones who are far, the young and the old, the sick and the able. We all had our beginning in God.

To dwell in the mystery of creation is to begin to understand that we should never take the earth for granted, should never take ourselves or any other person for granted. What is of such infinite, inestimable value should never be disposed of lightly or allowed to waste away.

This is not an economy in which only taxpayers or consumers matter; it is one in which everyone counts.

Suffice it to say that the economic principles that drive the culture of money are quite different from those that lie at the heart of the great economy of grace. In the taken-for-granted world of North American culture, economic and political strategies seem more driven by either greed or guilt. In the greedy hunt for more, there are many people who are simply tossed off as being of no account. Those who react against such consuming greed with a kind of vague liberal guilt may mitigate the social effects of such greed for a while but not in any radical way. Vague guilt seems ultimately powerless against the crass assertion that the culture of money is reality, the way things are and are meant to be.

Since the time of the Enlightenment, political thinkers have attempted to balance the freedom accorded in the marketplace with the rights of the individual and some sense of social responsibility. Abstract phrases such as "the dignity of the human person" had some compelling power as long as they were located within a culture that still retained some memory of the biblical origins of such a conviction—the vision of the creation of the world and each human person by a loving Creator who was the ultimate guarantee of goodness and dignity. However, when the ideals of liberal democracies lost a living connection with their biblical roots, those ideals no longer seemed so self-justifying. As a last resort, political thinkers had to turn to the principle of self-interest to justify social responsibility. It would be in everyone's self-interest, they argued, to alleviate the poverty that was at the root of so much crime and violence. They presumed that most people knew what was in their best self-interest and, knowing this, would work to achieve it.

In the culture of money, we see little evidence of a politics and economics of gratitude. The religious roots of such an attitude have withered and wasted away. More often than not, organized religion is used to justify the economics of greed or the politics of liberal guilt. The economics of gratitude exists as a partial memory of a time before the rise of capitalism, when notions such as the common good were compelling and vibrant. In the culture of money we tend to assume that capitalism in its present form is the only way of going about things. However, the possibility of an alternative exists as both memory and hope when we allow ourselves to admit the unhappiness that presently afflicts all in the culture of money.

We need the economic and political conditions that make it a little easier to be grateful. Religious people are summoned to sustain the imagination of another way of living economically. They are called to speak more about the WHY of economics rather than the HOW. It remains to economists, the professionals and those who are wise in the ways of the daily transaction of life, to work on the construction of the kind of economics that is more graceful than greedy.

Ingratitude

We are afflicted with ingratitude. Because we take the basic gift of life for granted, we can assume that our lives are, for better or for worse, what we have made of them. And we cannot look on what we have made and see that it is very good. On the way to getting something more, we fail to see what we have. We disregard what we step over on the way to somewhere else. We pay no attention to the person by our side on the way to someone else. We dismiss the good that we do on the way to something better.

This dissatisfaction afflicts the haves and the have-nots and those who have a little and want more.

The very rich may seem to have every reason to be grateful, yet this is not always the case. It may be even more difficult for them to experience the sheer gratuity of being loved for no reason. I remember visiting a very wealthy old aunt who was dying. After I had prayed with her, she reached over for her checkbook and asked me, almost automatically, whether I could use some money for one of my causes.

"No, I don't want any money," I responded—even to my own surprise. "I just came to see you and to be with you." Her eyes filled with tears. "I never know, you see, if someone is coming to see me just for myself or for my money." This gave me some insight into Jesus' remarks about how difficult it would be for the rich to enter the kingdom of God where love reigned, as difficult as it would be for a camel to pass through the eye of a needle. Very few love the rich for no reason, without self-interest, for free. The rich may hear words of gratitude, but they sound empty and ingratiating.

The difficulty the rich have in experiencing the gratuity of God's love may help explain contemporary theological talk about "the preferential option for the poor." I cannot imagine that this means God loves the poor more than the rich or the middle class. Such a qualification and quantification of God's love seems to reduce and restrict the mystery of God's all-encompassing love. The weigh-scales of our mind don't work well in this regard.

Nevertheless, it is just possible that the poor may have a special awareness of God's love because they have fewer illusions that they can earn the notice of others or can buy their affection and care.

For the truly destitute, it is much more difficult to be grateful. When one's entire existence hangs on the possibility of getting food or when generations of poverty have scarred not only the body but also the mind and spirit, then gratitude does not come easily. The destitute have reason to wonder whether one can get something for nothing. In other words, there are certain economic conditions that make it more difficult to experience the sheer gratuity of God's love. Not impossible, just much more difficult.

The restless striving that has earned them a place in the middle class afflicts those who neither have too much nor too little. By meeting the demands of becoming qualified and through personal sacrifice, they have internalized a sense that you can't get something for nothing. Having worked their way into an identity, they cannot imagine how the best things in life could possibly be for free and forever. Having neither too much nor too little, they can still remain dissatisfied with themselves.

Ingratitude is ingrained within every social class within the culture of money. It is how sin takes shape within us, conditions us, and holds us captive in many and various ways.

However, it must be said that gratitude for the gift of life cannot and should not mean that we must be grateful for everything in our lives. Gratitude does not dispel the mystery of suffering and evil in the world and may even deepen it. We cannot look at the child who has been raped and offer the theological maxim that God will draw something good from out of this. We cannot think of the children consumed by the fires of Auschwitz and Hiroshima and manufacture some easy gratitude. Gratitude does not take away the horrors of violence. Nevertheless, we become part of taking their lives for granted once again if we are not grateful for the fact that they once were alive. We can be grateful for the memory of their lives and maybe even grateful for the memory of why their deaths were so unnecessary and so evil.

The longer we live ungratefully, the more we strengthen the claims of a culture that takes everything and everyone for granted. We are creating the conditions in which we too may be taken for granted. As we take other people for granted, we will grow increasingly—although perhaps unconsciously—anxious about the possibility that we too will someday be taken for granted. In the culture of money there is no security for the poor or the rich or the middle class.

Ingratitude lies at the root of our difficulty in loving God beyond guilt and in loving others freely. It makes it more difficult to imagine a world in which it would be a little easier to be grateful.

Loving God for Nothing

To dwell in the wonder of our own creation, the "in our beginning," is to dwell intuitively in the mystery of the God who is the Creator of the world. This is the God whom the makers and shapers of modernity could not acknowledge because such acknowledgment would involve the fundamental admission that we human beings are indebted, in a most radical sense, for life.

We who live in a world shaped by the modern vision of human autonomy are often tempted to try to construct the world according to our own interests and even to manufacture or "make" our very selves. There are, for example, psychology books that emphasize the importance of working on yourself, working things through, doing dream work, doing deep work—as if the self were another thing, a commodity, that could be worked on and improved.

To be sure, there are things we can and should do to make ourselves a little better. All too often, however, this process of self-reconstruction leaves no room for wonder at our very origins—a reality for which we can take no credit. An acknowledgment of our origins will enable us to move far beyond the extremes of living in isolated independence or in unhealthy forms of dependent relationships. This is not easy to do in a culture that is simultaneously obsessed with independence and with forms of addiction and dependence. In recognizing our original and radical dependence on our Creator, we become freer to live in interdependent ways in which we become more truly who we are.

The self that we attempt to create is far more captivating than the self that is created. So too we are tempted to construct an image of God that suits our purposes. We fashion a god who can be wheeled out for state occasions or in times of national distress, or refashioned in politically correct or psychologically useful ways. Such a god is sometimes presented in our churches—the thoroughly manageable and predictable god. We don't really deny God (indeed, America is considered one of the most believing countries in the world), but we do tend to take God for granted.

When we stop taking God for granted and allow ourselves to be astonished at the unaccountable and priceless reality of God's love, then all the tidy little compartments of our contractual lives fall apart. When we can't add it all up, then begins the great spiritual awakening, the start of a mature spirituality. When we sense that God loves us for nothing, for no reason, we may begin to experience the desire to love God for no reason, neither expecting nor wanting anything in return. This is the beginning of the desire to pray and to worship simply because God is God.

Such a desire goes far beyond our calculations of the shoulds and oughts of contractual obligation and far beyond our needs and self-interest. It is a wanting and a willingness, the beginning of an adult faith in which we become like little children.

This side of the grave, such a desire to love God will surely always be mixed with some of our human needs and fears. We will always be tempted to define God in contractual terms. We will always be tempted to break the contract if we don't seem to be getting anything out of it. We will always be ungrateful.

Nevertheless, even though our desire to love God forever and for free is only intermittent, such moments are the most blessed in our lives. These are the moments of blessing and thanksgiving, the moments when we are set free from captivity to our calculations and cravings.

We worship because we hardly know how to say thanks for the most important realities in our lives—which are unearned, beyond our control, and given to us for free. We worship because we have a sense of having been blessed and, when we worship, our sense of being blessed deepens.

On the one hand, we worship because God is God and, on the other, we worship because we are who we are. We pray with the inexplicable sufferings and burdens in our lives. Sometimes we find the words with which to pray and sometimes we don't and it is at these moments that we are carried by the prayer of the worshipping community.

Eucharist

Within the Christian tradition, the Eucharist has become the great way of thanksgiving. It is the way in which we take our small and sometimes half-hearted acts of gratitude and join them with the total act of thanksgiving that Jesus was and is among us. He lived continually in the recognition that he had been born of God, that he was a child of God, and thus his life became a giving, a giving thanks, a blessing. In him our gratitude becomes whole, holy. In him our gratitude becomes free, good enough.

We lose the soul and meaning of worship when we make it yet another forum for old or new ideas or when we attempt to manage it according to our own interests. Priests, religious, and laity—we are all tempted in this regard.

I can predict that after I return from having attended church on Sunday, someone will always ask me, "What was it like?" This query usually means: What did you get out of it? Was it a good homily? How was the music? Was it politically correct?

My response to these spoken and unspoken questions is my little way of resisting the consumer approach to the Eucharist: "How was it? It was valid."

In making this response, I don't mean to dismiss some of the legitimate criticisms about the way worship services are conducted. Offensive words, empty gestures, and the inappropriate use of symbols can get in the way of worship. There are things in the church that must be changed so that it can become a place in which it is a little easier to be grateful.

Nevertheless, it is soul-destroying when discussions about the words and symbols of worship become a struggle to control, because the impetus to worship is based on something radically different from the need to control. Whether this need to control comes more from the clergy or from the people, it always diminishes and diverts the desire to worship.

The more obvious faults of the institutional church, such as the obvious need to control, can easily serve as a good excuse for abandoning the practice of going to church. There is so much that is less than perfect in the structures, symbols, words, and music used in worship services. However, we need to discern whether our dissatisfaction with the church is just that or whether it is part of the kind of general dissatisfaction with everything that is generated by the spirit of craving in the culture of money. The difference between specific dissatisfaction and a general sense of dissatisfaction becomes clearer if we are able to name some specific reasons why we are satisfied with worship, why it is "enough."

A certain freedom begins with the rather humble admission that none of our structures, symbols, or words will ever be adequate to express our desire to worship. Our words will always falter and our symbols will always conceal as much as they reveal. In short, our worship will never be good enough and yet it is enough, enough to begin, enough to go on.

Through the Eucharist, the great act of thanksgiving, we enter into the imagination of the great economy of grace. We know we are ungrateful and yet we also believe that our small gratefulness is gathered up and made holy in the name of Jesus. In entering into his memory and hope, we see a new way of being in which love and life are offered to all forever and for free. This is not merely a spiritual vision or one that is meant for Sunday alone. It is about bread and wine, loaves and fishes and feeding more than our souls and ourselves.

The Eucharist is also about imagining a different way of being in our weekday world. And it is about living during the week in ways that make it a little easier to celebrate Eucharist. Gratitude that is enclosed into only one area of our life or left in the realm of spirituality will not matter or make a difference in the world. Ultimately, such a restricted sense of gratitude will be consumed by the very world it would rather leave behind.

Giving Ourselves Away

When we realize how much we have been given—life, a beginning—we are moved, almost naturally it seems, to want to give away some of our things. Grateful people tend to give away their things, even their time and talents, and to become happier in the process. In giving away, the craving that holds us captive begins to loosen its grip. There is such a difference when living simply or serving others is done out of a spirit of gratitude rather than guilt. A given life is different from a driven life. Gratitude seems to replenish itself: as more is given, more is received. Guilt, in contrast, rather quickly exhausts itself in judgments.

Nevertheless, the most difficult possession to give away is ourselves. I remember listening to a much appreciated church worker assess her life as she lay dying. *I have given so much. I have given most of what I earned, all my time and talent...I have given everything except myself.* This thought was the source of profound guilt for her. She had not given enough and was dissatisfied with her life. I imagine that God was more sad than condemning, sad that she had not experienced the greatest happiness of all, that of giving yourself away.

There are probably as many ways of understanding the great economy of grace as there are people. Some, as I have suggested, may be so moved by the recognition of what they have been given that they may begin to give freely of themselves. Others may come to understand the free gift of God's love through their practical experience of loving other people.

This way is forcefully delineated by Dostoevsky in the story of the encounter between "the woman of little faith" and the holy monk Father Zosima in *The Brothers Karamazov.*

The woman has come to see the holy monk because she has been suffering from doubts about the existence of God. Father Zosima tells her that he cannot prove the existence of God but that it is possible to be convinced. *By the practice of active love.*

He explains what this means. "Try to love your neighbors actively and tirelessly. The more you succeed in loving, the more you'll be convinced of the existence of God and the immortality of your soul. And if you attain real complete selflessness in the love of your neighbor, then undoubtedly you will believe and no doubt will even be able to enter your soul. This has been tested. It is certain."

The woman replies that she has moments when she dreams of giving up all that she has and becoming a sister of mercy but she knows that there is one thing she could not handle and that would be the ingratitude of those whom she seeks to serve.

Father Zosima tells her that "love in dreams thirsts for immediate action, quickly performed, and with everyone watching. Indeed, it will go as far as the giving even of one's life, provided it does not take too long but is over as on stage, and everyone is looking on and praising. Whereas love in action is a harsh and dreadful love."

What the holy monk is saying, I think, is that if we are able to continue to live gratefully and generously even (and especially) when we receive nothing in return, then we will come to a new understanding of the divine nature of love—which continues unabated even as God is often taken for granted and treated with ingratitude. It is similar to what may happen to a new mother overwhelmed with love for her child—at that moment she may just realize how much her own mother must have loved her.

Gratitude may move us to giving, but giving may also lead us to a deeper sense of gratitude.

When we cease taking life for granted, our own life or the life of another, we may begin to realize the awesome responsibility we have for providing a guarantee for life. Being grateful does not mean letting life slip through our hands or treating it as a commodity doomed to obsolescence. To dwell in gratitude is to begin to recognize that other people are not simply objects to be disposed of or even objects of our concern. We do not make or break other people but we may act as a guarantee for their lives. Such guarantees may be provided in the simplest and most complex ways. They may be ensured by a cup of coffee or by a more equitable economic system. Thus, gratitude may involve doing our part to provide the kind of social and political or even legal guarantees to ensure that human life is not treated as a cheap grace. It may even involve giving our own life so that it becomes the guarantee for the life of another.

Jesus, the Example of Radical Gratitude

In the person of Jesus, we see the example of what it means to live in radical gratitude. Examples serve us when we do not know how to define what we mean by something as profound as radical gratitude. In the life of Jesus we see someone whose life gave weight to his words.

Jesus knew that he had been born of God, that he was a child of God. In understanding his origin, he also discovered that he was with God and that this was his particular form of power. In knowing he had come from God, he also believed that he was going to God, the point of his being.

The recognition that he had been born of God led him freely and simply to give—to give of himself and of his things. He has shown us the way of the loaves and fishes, when what we give away multiplies, ignites, and sustains. He has shown us how one good word grows and gathers into a symphony of truth. He has shown us how one small hope whispered in the dark fills out and flows until it becomes a movement. He has spoken about the lilies of the field who neither work nor worry and are blessed in doing nothing and who bless by being just lilies. He has shown us the way of the supper when you set the table with your life and it becomes as real as love, friendship, and community.

And...he gave his life as a guarantee for our lives. He told us that we should never take for granted our own life or that of another. Those who had been most taken for granted, the poor and the outcasts, he accounted as being of infinite value. He did not simply let his life be wasted away, but rather he gave of it freely, fully, and forever.

One of his most radical teachings had to do with forgiveness. It is such a difficult teaching that it can easily be trivialized. It can, for example, be used to dispose of the consequences of our actions in an easy sort of way. Forgiving and forgetting is simply another form of spiritual consumerism. What Jesus taught is that our actions and intentions have weight; for better or worse they make a difference in the world. He did not ask children to simply forgive and forget the wrongs that had been done to them; he did not ask innocent victims just to forgive and forget criminals; he did not ask us just to forgive and forget the wrongs we ourselves have done.

In his words and in his actions, he tied forgiveness to the mystery of beginning again. Forgiveness was meant to be not a denial of the past, but a way of guaranteeing that the past would not simply repeat itself again and again in the present and in the future. Through forgiveness, the new beginning, the cycle of from bad to worse can be broken.

Acting on Gratitude

Still. Nevertheless, will we act on the sense of gratitude, which we sometimes recognize in our moments of liberation? Can we sustain our sense of astonishment at the miracle of life in a culture that so easily takes life for granted? Do we really believe we will be set free from the chains of dissatisfaction once we realize how tightly we are held captive? These questions arise from the sense of powerlessness, which is intrinsic to the culture of perpetual dissatisfaction and can be answered only from a more profound and positive sense of the creative power that is intimately linked to a sense of gratitude.

Gratitude is the beginning of our faith and hope in the possibility of creating something new in the world, of becoming someone new.

———————————

We are grateful.
You have given us this day
and have given us this way
to say Thank You.

We thank you for giving us
what we need to be grateful.
We offer back to You
   all that we have
   all that we are.
We know our thank you
is as fragile as we are
—it can be crushed
   by the care of the moment
—it can disappear
   in the heat of the day
—it can be blown away
   by the winds of suffering.

And so we ask You
to take our small thank you
into Your great act of Thanksgiving:
You, Lord of the loaves and fishes,
You who are from God
with God and for God,
You in whom it is all
Yes and Amen.

CHAPTER FOUR

Creative Power

Fire of our fire
You leap between us
and among us
Light traveling at night
signaling in the distance
Spark of hope
and warm gathering of love
Ignite the hope
that sleeps among us
Enkindle the power
stacked between our wooden lives
Stir the embers
of Your blessed joy.

Gratitude begins as small and as real as a child. It enters the world as wonder as simple as a flower.

Yet, there are children who never see themselves through the eyes of gratitude, there are flowers mowed down on the way to someone else's fairway or highway. How can gratitude grow up and walk sure in the world? Can it survive only in an incubator or in some hot house of spirituality? Is it only for a season or in the garden of one's life? Is it possible after September 11?

There are times and places when gratitude seems as small and weak as a child, as vulnerable as a jasmine plant in the poisonous green smoke, as unreal as the possibility of the great economy of grace in the world. Such are the temptations to powerlessness in America, the North and the West, in a time of endings and beginnings. Thus, the tendency to think of gratitude as a lifestyle reserved for the few who have their mountaintop hideaway while most must work, even slave, in the valley below.

If we are not convinced that what we do or say really makes a difference in the world, then spirituality will become another attempt at escapism and work a dispirited form of activism.

The desire to escape from the treadmill of work, from the all-consuming effort to exist, motivates an increasing number of people to look for a place of retreat or a vacation to get away from it all. Nevertheless, an escape is not yet liberation. If we simply return to the drivenness of life, then the memory of such escapes will serve only to deepen our dissatisfaction with life without providing any way through or beyond the patterns of captivity in this culture. It is even possible that the desire for such escapes will only further strengthen the chains that hold us captive. We may simply be driven to work harder and longer to be able to make even more escapes.

Such a pattern of escape and return will continue as long as we remain convinced that gratitude as an attitude is rather powerless to effect any change in the real world in which we live, a world governed by powerful economic and political interests over which we seem to have little or no control. To make the world a place in which it would be a little easier to be grateful seems so impossible that it is understandable why some people would move toward trying to change the only world they can, the inner world of the self. The search for inner power then becomes a way of surviving the powers that be in the world. Survival is a long way away from liberation; it is the choice not to die but not yet the choice to live.

The underlying sense of powerlessness in such an effort can be illustrated in an advertisement for Second Debut, a skin moisturizer. Beautiful Catherine Deneuve leans forward on the television screen and suggests that "If you can't change the world you can at least change your moisturizer."

Liberation then would mean going beyond the concepts of power and powerlessness that hold us captive, beyond the forced extremes of powerless love or power exercised without love. It would mean developing an understanding of the intrinsic link between gratitude and a more creative sense of power.

The Craving for Power

Throughout the course of Western history, power has been understood in many and various ways. Unlike a mathematical idea, it is not easy to define, and indeed the British philosopher Bertrand Russell called it one of the most "slippery" concepts. In general, it has been seen as the ability to get what you want or, as the ancient thinkers said, to realize your potential. Getting power and keeping it has been associated with physical prowess, with military force, with economic heft, with political or cultural influence, or with the authority associated with certain positions. It is sometimes attributed to individuals and at other times to groups. Rarely do we think that an idea, such as truth, has power.

Whatever the case, power has been seen as something both to be desired and to be feared. It is to be feared when the desire for power becomes a craving for more power, a craving for power for the sake of power. The person to be feared would be someone like Howard Hughes who, if asked how much power would be enough, would respond *just a little bit more*. How rare the person or the nation who looks at the power in hand and says: it is enough.

This craving for power has been increasingly associated in modern times with the acquisition of knowledge and information. This modern version of how the world can be changed has shaped America more than any place else on earth. If the vision of modernity is shaken, its tremors will be felt here as a shaking of the foundations.

The Enlightenment thinkers inaugurated a new faith in the power of reason, in the dignity and rights of the individual, and in the ideal of freedom as liberty from the constraints imposed by various forms of "external" power. The rational arguments of the Enlightenment laid the foundation for the noble ideals of democracy and human rights through their critique of various forms of demonic or divine imperialism. In the process, the Enlightenment thinkers, for better and for worse, questioned many of the treasured notions of tradition, authority, and community.

The scientific method was based on a belief in knowledge as a superior way of participating in reality, far more accurate and trustworthy than feeling and believing. Relying on observation, categorization, hypothesis, and verification, this method delivered a very certain kind of power. It was the power to understand, to predict, and thus to control the world. Surprise was an attitude to be eliminated. Astonishment and awe, faith and trust were consigned to those who had not yet learned how the world worked. Those who could tried to explain away the persistence of fear, love, and hope beyond reason, the desire to worship and the wonderment of life.

Knowledge became the new source of power and the instruments and technology of science became new tools of power. The world was seen as an object, as a machine, which could be analyzed, broken down into component parts, and reconstructed in better ways. So too, human beings were seen as the objects of scientific research—objects that could be analyzed, catalogued, and rehabilitated—either psychologically or sociologically. More recently they have become the information bits in a new program of analysis.

Thus, the modern world has cultivated within us a curious and conflicting experience of power. On the one hand, we imagine that we have mastery or power over the world and, on the other, we experience ourselves as merely parts of some great machine or system that can be manipulated and controlled by others. Modernity simultaneously generates images of human beings as all-powerful and nearly powerless.

This approach to the world belonged not only to scientists and technicians but eventually became an attitude that pervades most of Western culture. We presume that we can work on the world and on ourselves and that we can improve both.

The modern view of the world is also at the root of our perpetual dissatisfaction—it takes so much for granted. The world becomes something to be manufactured and constructed rather than something to be created, much less recognized as God's creation. It is a world in which we should feel like gods but in which, more often than not, we feel like cogs in a machine or flickers of light struggling to stay on the screen before they are deleted.

Middle-class people, people who are trained through information and technology, experience this dilemma acutely. They know enough to think they should be more in control of the world and they know enough to know they are not in control. The very poor, on the other hand, know quite clearly that they are not in control of their own lives or anyone else's.

It must be said that there have been and are great thinkers whose pursuit of scientific knowledge has led them to an ever-deeper awe at the mystery of creation, to an astonishment at some of the great unpredictabilities in the world. Yet, for every one of these wondering thinkers, there have been many more who have toiled away in the belief that with just enough know-how and can-do, the surprise and unpredictabilities of life, all the seeming irrationalities of life, could be eliminated.

Fortunately, more knowledge has indeed helped us to deal with some of the irrationalities of life. Psychological insights have seemed to tame some of the torments which had appeared to be either irrational or even demonic. Sociological and anthropological research has helped us understand and even address some of the insanities in the social order. Children are vaccinated, some of the blind do see again, and all the wisdom of past centuries is more available to more people than ever before.

However, with hindsight we can also see that the faith in the power of reason to solve all problems was indeed a blind faith, an unproven faith, based largely on the need to predict and control. Reason did give us a measure of control over some aspects of our lives, but it also unleashed the depravities associated with the insatiable need to control. The irrationality of the all-consuming need to control the world, efficiently and effectively, exploded in the twentieth century in places such as Auschwitz and Hiroshima.

It was this blind faith in reason that repressed not only awe and gratitude but also profound questions about the persistence of evil, about the nature of evil that could not be explained—evil done for the sake of evil. In the twenty-first century we are finding it hard to think about what we are, nonetheless, able to do.

Power and Controlling Interest

Day by day, we try to get our lives a little more under control, try to make our very taken-for-granted world more predictable. At the same time, we crave for novelty and for the latest and the best, but only within a very narrow range of social expectations. We want to be stimulated but not surprised, novelty but not genuine newness, a lifestyle more than a life. In a pinch, we will consult astrologers and the stars to get a better fix on things.

Our culture, which seems so progressive and trendy, is, nonetheless, resistant to change and lacking in true creativity because of its inherent suspicion of the unknown, the uncontrollable. Thus, while we can tinker at politics and economics, the great economy of grace seems much too elusive and unpredictable to think about.

The pollsters are the new high priests, those who attempt to predict and control the future in a desperate attempt to domesticate the unknown. The fear of the unpredictabilities of the future has spawned a whole industry of consultants who specialize in "visioning" and "long term planning." Their authority is as strong and unquestioned as our desire to control the future. The knowledge elites, the professionals and managers and experts, use increasingly complex language that serves as a means of protection and control.

Thus, it is virtually impossible for an ordinary person to go to court to explain in simple terms why he or she is not guilty. A lawyer must be hired to speak in terms that only the judge and other lawyers can understand. We rely on psychologists to tell us what is "normal," on the chattering classes to tell us what is hot and what is not, on professional feminists to tell us what liberation means, and on economists to tell us what we must inevitably and realistically expect.

When knowledge becomes the dominant form of power, controlling access to information becomes crucial. Knowing "secrets" about a person, an organization, a trend can be a potent source of power. Conversely, withholding information or misusing it can become a new form of social crime or sinfulness.

New people on the block often bear the brunt of this excessive fear of the unknown. I recall the furious little face of a friend's son. The little boy had just been disciplined and the worst possible threat he could hurl at his mother was this: "I'm going to go out," he said, "and talk to strangers."

The fear of the stranger, the refugee, the immigrant, the new kid on the block is inherent within this modern idealization of power as control. Those who act in different and unpredictable ways, who speak a language we do not understand, who have not yet fit into our scheme of things, present a threat.

It is no accident, I think, that the great moral issues of our day are issues of control. There is the issue of the control of birth, either through contraceptives or abortion, and the new fashion in designer children. There are the acute and pressing issues of the control of death through euthanasia or assisted suicide.

The much-discussed case of Sue Rodriguez in Canada is a case in point. A member of Parliament, Svend Robinson, who had fought for her right to have an assisted suicide, was with her when she died. Talking to the press afterwards, an emotional Robinson said with great pride: "She was totally in control right up to the moment of her death." His point, I take it, is that we should manage death better so we won't get out of control.

As the world seems increasingly beyond our control, especially after September 11, self-control becomes a personal and social ideal. Interestingly enough, people who would never undertake some of the more traditional forms of discipline (such as fasting) willingly undertake diets and exercise as ways of maintaining some control over their bodies. Self-knowledge is often seen as the key to self-control. The self is seen as an object over which, if you just think hard enough and work smart enough, you will have some control. Consider the number of self-help books that offer advice on "working" on yourself.

Within this context, an important virtue is taking responsibility for your life—which means having control over the consequences of your actions and intentions. Ultimately, the ethic of control is the logical and bodily extension of the capitalist mindset, which reduces all of reality to private property and believes that all property should be (rationally) controlled by its owner.

Being out of control is a fate that seems almost worse than death. We want people who are addicted to get their lives under control. Women defend their right to control their bodies as zealously as any capitalist would defend the right to control his property. We want society to institutionalize people like young offenders and criminals who are out of control. We have ominous thoughts when the elderly tremble and the disabled shake—because they are so out of control.

Of course, such an ideal of near-total control of one's own life, let alone the lives of others or the world, is an impossible dream. It inevitably generates feelings of deep powerlessness because it is based on an all-or-nothing wager: Either you are totally in control or you are powerless. Yet, how many could feel totally in control? In control of all the facts? All the outcomes? It is perhaps this impossible ideal of power that has blinded so many of us in our culture to the more limited but real forms of power that we have.

The sense of dissatisfaction generated by the cravings of consumerism and the impossible ideal of control dictated by the ideals of the Enlightenment combine in North America to hold us captive and powerless. When will we ever have enough knowledge and information to act? When will we ever be together enough to realize true liberation in our lives? For middle-class people, these questions are particularly difficult. From time to time we know we are not happy, but because we do not seem to be dying or poor, we just continue to cope.

It makes it difficult for us to ask what or how much we really need to feel some sense of control in our lives. How much control is enough? How much would satisfy us? Beyond the extreme ideal of being totally in control or the extreme feeling of being totally out of control we all need to have some modicum of control in our lives. We need to know where the next meal is coming from, we need a roof over our heads, and we need to be able to walk down the street without fear. Without these we are definitely powerless.

Yet, we also need to live with mysterious realities that are beyond our control. We need love and friendship, a sense of meaning and purpose in our lives, and a reason to hope. These we cannot manufacture or control. These involve risk and a willingness to venture into the unknown.

The world we seek to control tends to shrink. It can only become a small, dark space—perhaps the size of a safety deposit box or a coffin.

Powerlessness Corrupts

Liberation from the ties that bind us involves an aching recognition of how deeply powerless we feel to bring about any change in our lives or in the lives of others. Such a sense of powerlessness, as I have mentioned in chapter two, may be evidenced in either a sense of paralysis or in the frantically busy life. We know how to tinker at life but hardly believe that we will ever be able to bring about any significant change.

The recognition may come in the aching—in the aching desire to help someone we love, in the aching in the midst of profound injustice, in the aching memories of those moments when we knew we were grateful and free. We knew what we wanted to do or what we had to do and yet we felt powerless to do it. In short, we experience the aching recognition of our captivity. Awareness of the cost of such captivity may come in a personal realization at the middle or end of one's life or in the shared social realization at the end of an era—all the hopes that remained unrealized, all the gifts that were ground down and tossed away as impossible dreams, all the children we took for granted who now turn on us and take us for granted.

The old adage is that "power corrupts and absolute power corrupts absolutely." This is doubtless true, especially with regard to power exercised in a dominating and controlling way. Yet it is also true that "powerlessness corrupts" in ways that are less obvious but equally disastrous, not only for oneself but for society as a whole. It destroys dreams, leaves people consumed with jealousy and resentment, makes violence more possible.

Michael Lerner, who was active in the anti-war movement of the sixties, was struck by how many people in the protest movement, in spite of all their rhetoric about empowerment, had a deep-seated will to lose. Because they were not really convinced of their own ability to make any change, because they felt deeply powerless, they often acted in ways that sabotaged their own stated ideals. Those who had a will to lose became losers.

I have seen this deep-seated sense of powerlessness in far too many groups and individuals who are apparently committed to social change. There are groups that struggle for justice, that organize to help empower "the powerless" who are somehow other people out there, not us. In effect, "the powerless" persist within the group itself, sabotaging any imagination or conviction of the possibility of success. And so, in spite of all the efforts made in a particular campaign, someone forgets to bring the microphone to the closing rally, someone puts the wrong address on the flyer advertising the rally, and someone forgets to pick up the guest speaker. These are not "irresponsible" actions. These are the actions of people who do not really believe that they can make a difference and that their actions matter. And, because they don't believe their actions will make a difference, they don't.

Each one of us can recall listening to speeches during which we tuned out or nodded off. It wasn't always for lack of interest on our part or even for lack of a good idea on the speaker's part. Sometimes it was just the tonality of the whole speech—the lack of conviction, the sense that the speaker didn't really believe that what he or she was saying really mattered. The speaker went on speaking, but in ways that in fact ensured no one would listen.

The problem with a sense of powerlessness is that it becomes a self-fulfilling prophecy.

Many of our cultural institutions tend to reinforce this sense of powerlessness. It happens early on in families. A child screams, but the mother or father is too tired or too busy to respond and the child internalizes a sense that screaming won't make a difference.

In school, children are taught to adjust to what is called "reality." Through countless examples, stories from history, and lessons in life, students absorb how it was, how it is and how it must be. The numbness of normal. Politicians give rather predictable speeches about what is realistic and possible: *Sure there are problems, but consider the alternative.* Within the churches, there are those who will counsel accepting life as it happens *because it is God's will.*

Dreams Deferred

There are elements of truth in this broad education into "reality." Part of maturing means coming to terms with what is realistic and possible. It means letting go of *some* dreams. There are certain dreams, such as the dreams of Prince Charming on the Starship Enterprise, which we can and must let go of. But should we let go of *all* dreams because we feel so powerless to make them real? The craving for more grows as the dream of something different, someone truly different, dies.

The woman washing dishes looks out her kitchen window and thinks about all her life going down the drain. *I want to stop*, she thinks but she can't stop—or so she thinks—and so she continues washing cup after empty cup.

The man glances over at his desk. He sees the picture of his kids and then reaches for his date book to pencil them in, but not in ink, not yet, not until he checks his e-mail, which he must do—or so he thinks—and so he does.

In the coffee hour after the church service, someone wonders out loud whether the lawn by the side of the building could be turned into a community garden for the neighbors. No sooner has she said it than someone says what she was already thinking: That is where they always take the wedding pictures.

Meanwhile, over at the soup kitchen, someone finally says what everyone has been thinking: "We are sick of peanut butter and pasta and we should ask the mayor to try eating this stuff for a week." The silence rings for a moment and then someone yells, "He should eat dirt!" Haw, haw, haw down the ever-lengthening line.

For want of a sense of power, the dream of something new and someone different dies. When we don't believe we can make any difference, some small part of God's dream for the world dies.

The Resentment of Powerlessness

Resentment grows like bitter weeds in the soil of powerlessness. Cynicism, jealousy, envy, hatred, and fantasies of revenge. Bitter weeds that grow when people no longer have any conviction that they can change their particular circumstances of life. Bitter weeds that choke off small seeds of hope in a society. Bitter weeds that choke on themselves.

The truth about resentment is that it craves what it says that it detests. Resentment not only signifies powerlessness but also ensures that it will continue. Resentment will never create the possibility of something new, but can lead only to destruction.

North America today is seething with resentment. How could this not be when the culture of money is saturated with images of people who have more, who do more, who enjoy more? Poverty here is not usually very ennobling and one can wax eloquent about its virtues only from a distance.

Someone like Karl Marx may have thought that the sight of the young and the restless and the bold and the beautiful would move the poor to revolt for justice. In truth, the world of the soap operas becomes both a source of resentment and a means of escape. When a better life seems only an advertisement away, the passion for change is twisted into resentment and illusion. The armchair coaches, the armchair politicians, and the wanna-be stars have everything to say about the people they watch but little to do. They enjoy the spectacle of the public unhappiness of the rich and famous but secretly wish they could be so unhappy.

The cynicism about public figures, big money, and big corporations comes easy to the middle class as well. They have lots to say about this and sometimes they say it very well. However, as long as we secretly crave to be just like the people we so vocally detest, it won't make any difference in the end.

Powerlessness corrupts. Powerlessness may destroy, but it will never create.

Powerlessness and Violence

Of those who feel they have little or no control over their lives, there are some who will inevitably turn to violence. We tend to think that most of the violence in the world takes place through the exercise of power. While it is true that terrible violence often attends the use of what could more appropriately be called force, it is also true that violence often arises from a sense of powerlessness. The desire to be totally in control and the feeling of being totally out of control can lead, in different ways, to violence.

More than ten years ago, a young man called Marc Lepine walked into the Ecole Polytechnique in Montreal and shot fourteen young women. Those who pieced together the story of his life after this event did not unearth some fire-breathing chauvinist. He emerged as an ordinary guy who felt quite powerless over most aspects of his life.

The Oklahoma bomber and the student who pulled the trigger at Columbine High School in the United States were also, by all accounts, social misfits. The profile of the powerless and violent attacker of innocent people is repeated again and again in the terrifying eruptions of random violence throughout North America.

Similarly, we find a high degree of violence in communities and families where the adults, mostly adult men, experience themselves as powerless in their work and in the society in which they live.

Oppressed groups who have long been denied any access to legitimate and effective forms of participation in the political process will frequently resort to violence in a desperate attempt to bring about some change. Those who have little or no control over their own existence can be driven to take ultimate control over their own lives and the lives of others. We should not be surprised.

The Enchantment of Powerlessness

Nevertheless, powerlessness still remains an attractive option for some, if not many. There is a moral high ground to be claimed by powerless victims. It is a place where you do not have to take responsibility for power.

The groundwork for this position was laid out in the long course of the Christian tradition, a tradition that still shapes some of our cultural norms and values around the use and abuse of power.

Early on, Christian attitudes toward power were shaped by the political realities of the empire in which Christians lived. As a persecuted minority, they experienced power as nothing but oppressive and domineering. When Christianity eventually became the established religion of the Empire and after Rome fell, Christians who had experienced power as so negative and corrupt began to see powerlessness as the virtuous alternative. It should be noted that it was men of good will who, recognizing the pitfalls of power within themselves and their culture, articulated many of these spiritualities. Needless to say, such spiritualities only accentuated the already powerless position of women in the culture and in the church.

At the time of the Protestant Reformation, this suspicion of power within the political realm and within the church itself only deepened. Through original sin, so the reformers believed, the inner structure of the human being had not only been weakened but also severely corrupted. Thus the exercise of political power was seen as inevitably destined for corruption. The Protestant spirit eventually found a worldly foothold in the political shape of liberal democracy and in the economic form of capitalism. In these political and economic models, there was a minimalizing of the extent to which authority or power could be exercised over the free will and autonomy of the individual.

In sum, the exercise of power inevitably involved responsibility and guilt, whereas powerlessness implied innocence.

The Innocence of Victims

If we recall the vague free-floating guilt that is so prevalent in the culture of dissatisfaction, then it is not too difficult to see why the innocent status of the powerless victim is something we would all like to lay claim to.

Indeed, it is a status that many, even the seemingly powerful, claim to hold. One hears politicians portraying themselves (and their supporters) as victims who have no choice but to cut taxes or to increase taxes because "the economy" demands it and they have very little power over the economics of the new global order. All we can do, they say, is simply adjust and manage as best as we can. Different political interest groups lament that they are being ripped off and cheated by other interest groups. Lobby groups portray themselves as victims of some vast right-wing or left-wing conspiracy. The heads of corporations present themselves as help-less servants of a new economy that forces them, against their will, to slash and burn jobs and to move plants to some freer trade zone.

In this headlong rush to avoid responsibility, a lot of people present themselves, to themselves and others, as being victimized by something or someone. As a result, the category of "victim" has become so broad as to be almost meaningless.

The situation is further complicated by the number of groups constituted around victims' rights—each group trying to ensure its rights on the basis of having been wronged. In my opinion this is a very dangerous strategy and very fragile basis for ensuring rights, because the sense of being wronged must be perpetuated. Even when some of those wrongs have ceased to exist, if persecutors cannot be found, new oppressors must be created so that the status of victimhood can be sustained. The blame must be perpetuated. The position of victim seems to provide the basis for claiming rights and the basis for presuming one's moral innocence.

I became painfully aware of this situation some years ago when I attended a symposium in Washington, D.C., on victims of the Holocaust. Group after group made presentations seemingly de-signed to prove that they had been the most victimized by the Nazis: the gypsies, the Jews, the Marxists, the gays. I found the quantification and categorization of suffering appalling. I felt the genuine victimization of real people was being used to score politi-cal points.

In bookstores all across the United States and Canada, we have shelves upon shelves of pop psychology analysis that can pro-vide just about everyone with a justification for calling oneself a victim. These psychologies allow us to name either society or someone else as the villain. This allows us to assume some posi-tion of innocence and moral superiority and can lead to a great deal of emotional manipulation in personal relationships. It also makes it much harder to see the real victims of persecution and can become a way of obscuring the real violence of a society.

In the end, using the status of victim as a way of claiming rights or moral superiority is a risky venture indeed and does little to ensure justice for real victims. If a "victim" is once seen to be wrong, is ever seen as less than pure and innocent, ever makes a mistake or turns out to be thoroughly obnoxious—then that is reason enough to deny him or her rights and respect. The fact is that people have rights because they are human beings, children of God. Rights have nothing to do with whether people are victims or not, nice or not, clean or smelly, employed or unemployed, men or women.

We are deluged with the rhetoric of victimhood and it is obscuring some of the disturbing realities in our society. When the banks and governments say they are victims of a global economy, when school trustees feel victimized by the government and teachers feel they are scapegoated in the process, then something is amiss. When everyone is a victim, then no one is. When everyone is a powerless victim, then everyone is innocent. And, more significantly, no one is responsible. Gone is the sense of ethical responsibility and moral agency. How easily we could all claim to be victims of the culture of perpetual dissatisfaction!

The Organization of Powerlessness

Let me recall our modest efforts to turn the house for a car into a room for a person. In order to change the function of our garage we had to go to City Hall. Nobody seemed to have the power to do anything to help us. When we went to the clerks at the point of entry into the system, they said they couldn't do anything except follow the rules. When we went to the people who seemed to be in the middle and at the top, they claimed they were equally helpless to alter the situation. Nobody seemed to be in control. This is how powerlessness is organized within our culture, in bureaucracies and networks of power.

The outlines of bureaucracy began to take shape to meet the needs of modern capitalism and technology. As an organizational form it generated both the appearance of efficiency and the reality of inefficiency, the appearance of power and the experience of powerlessness for those who worked within it. It was a structure that would eventually allow almost everyone in it to claim moral innocence.

In my experience of trying to bring about some change within specific systems, I have found that it is very difficult to identify who can actually be held responsible for some of the problems that exist. Those at the top and in the middle often seem to feel as powerless as those at the bottom. The neat old line between oppressor and oppressed becomes quite blurred within the modern forms of bureaucratic organization in which those who could be called oppressors often feel quite oppressed by a system over which they seem or claim to have little control and in which those who claim to be oppressed seem to be very much implicated in their own oppression—simply by participating in the system.

When I see the systematic organization of a simultaneous sense of guilt and innocence, I recall some ancient medieval paintings in which the devil was presented without a face, the faceless one, the Nobody. There could be something demonic in systems which make everyone feel slightly guilty but nobody feels responsible or able to do anything about it.

This vague sense of guilt and responsibility is intensified, I think, in the newer forms of organization that attend the development of the new information-based economy. When workers move from contract to contract, seldom seeing any cumulative effect of their labors, then the disconnection from the consequences of one's work only intensifies.

Within networks of organization and information, consultants and managers move in and out and sideways with increasing fluidity. The sense of responsibility and power becomes more and more diffuse as it becomes more difficult to identify who is really in charge at the moment. Without any clear sense of who or what could be responsible for the dehumanizing nature of the work, it becomes difficult to rebel. People float in a sea of information, unable to understand the organization that keeps them afloat.

The employee or consultant must identify totally with the interests of the company, knowing at every moment that he or she or the whole company could be deleted, merged, or acquired in some new combination of interests. The solidity of any sense of power and responsibility disappears in such an organizational form.

In summary, within the culture of money and technology we crave power and control even as we remain constantly dissatisfied with the limited but real power that we do have. In searching for more control, we are left with a feeling of near total powerlessness, with a sense that we cannot make any difference in the world. Indeed, in the social organization of our lives, many institutions and networks only reinforce that sense of powerlessness.

Dare we hope for liberation if we seem so powerless? Not until we discover a new sense of power, one more intimately linked to a sense of gratitude than to a feeling of dissatisfaction and the craving for control. We need some basis for believing that power may be as creative as it is destructive.

Relational Power

Underneath all of the considerations of power and powerlessness that I have explored thus far is a very solid and flat concept. These reflections have presumed, as many normally do in their daily lives, that power is something that can be measured and quantified—something like a pie that can be divided up in various portions.

If we tend to imagine power as a pie, either very big or very little, then we tend to think in terms of some having more and others less. One person's gain is another's loss. Where dissatisfaction reigns supreme, as it does in our culture, then the scene is set for a conflict over the pie. Only the whole pie will suffice; nothing else will satisfy. It becomes an all-or-nothing proposition in which even a little bit of power will never seem enough.

This pie in our eye blinds us and keeps us from seeing that power may not be like a pie at all.

If we were to follow the insights of scientists such as Einstein, then we would be more inclined to think of power as energy, as the light and heat arcing between two poles, as the energy that exists within each atom and between all the molecules of the universe. Everything in the world pulsates with energy.

This simple shift in our imagination, from power as a measurable thing to power as an almost immeasurable energy, has enormous political and even spiritual implications. It leads us to think about the conditions that would activate such potential energy.

If power is not a thing, then it cannot be possessed and retained by a solitary individual. It is activated only when at least two or three are gathered, when some or many people come together and interact. In other words, it exists only when the fabric of human relationship is activated and it ceases to exist when people are isolated or dispersed. In other words, the solitary individual, whether rich or poor, has little or no power. Power emerges and becomes active when people interact, discuss, debate, and even disagree.

Power, in other words, emerges in the interrelatedness of life. It exists in the in-between of life. This is why small groups of people who have engaged in an intense interaction have had power and the energy for change out of all proportion to their numbers. It is also why many people who remain in isolation from one another have made little difference in the world.

I see this relational model of power as both promising and problematic. It does open up the possibility that people may gather in the hope of making a world in which it is a little bit easier to be grateful. It means that there could be a power for change that could liberate us from the captivity of dissatisfaction. Yet, there is nothing automatic about this for everything depends on if and how people relate to one another and whether they do so for the good.

The potential in such a relational model of power has been recognized for some time by feminist thinkers. Because they characterize women as more relational, they understand the potential for a new understanding of power. They recognize that power may have less to do with money and weapons and positions of authority than with the quality of relationships formed between people.

However, it would be naive to think that human interaction is always for the good, always better than isolated individualism. This is not necessarily the case. People can keep each other under surveillance, can hold each other in check through their relationships. Not all relationships are healthy and some groups are paralyzed by dynamics that are decidedly unhealthy. Small groups of people, highly organized and effective, have also seized power only to wreak great destruction.

Power, which is actualized in human relations, can be for the better or for the worse. If power arises through interaction, it moves beyond the control of any one person. This means that I am never totally in control of all the consequences of my action. There may be results, good or bad, that I may never have intended. For example, I may initiate a small project that may grow in influence beyond anything I could possibly have imagined. Or, I may give someone a gift that may be misused and may lead to some disastrous consequences. I remember listening to a politician who told me, with tears in his eyes, that he had promised to give his son a bike for his birthday and he kept that promise. The next day his son rode the bike for the first time and was struck by a car and killed.

In the interconnectedness of power, I may become part of something greater and grander, such as the "communion of saints" in the Christian tradition; this is to be celebrated. Yet, it is also true that I may willingly or unwillingly and unconsciously become part of something dangerous and disastrous.

The awareness of the potential for such a relational model of power has animated some of the newer spiritualities that recognize the importance of connecting not merely with other people but with the energy of the universe. This deep sense of interconnectedness offers the beginning of a profound alternative to the modern view of the world. Indeed, it offers a form of self-transcendence that may well replace the forms of self-transcendence that have been associated with nation building.

However, obliterating the boundary between the self and the cosmos is not without its problems. One possibility is that the cosmos may come crashing in on the self, leaving it without any sense of identity or power; the other possibility is that the self may become increasingly narcissistic, projecting all its needs and wants onto the vast screen of the cosmos.

There are particularly challenging questions when the vague feeling of being connected to the universe does not translate into energizing relationships for change in the world. It is challenging for political organizers who must entice powerless people out of their sense of isolation. And no group is more isolated than those in the so-called middle class who have been educated into being self-reliant individuals. They have gone to school and earned their stripes alone. Their process of qualification demands that they take exams alone and graduate with a sense of having made it on their own. We are educated out of our need for community and, indeed, the skills we learn in postsecondary education make us particularly unfit for functioning in community, leaving us vulnerable to an isolated sense of powerlessness.

What makes the difference between the power that is related to good and the power that is related to evil? The question revolves around another dimension of relationship, the ultimacy of personal relationships. Are we ultimately related to Somebody or to Nobody? To whom or to what do we give ultimate power in our lives?

The Omnipotence of God

We have called You names.
We have cut you down
   to our smaller size.
We cannot bear not knowing
   who You are.
We cannot stand not knowing
   what You will do next.
We, the managers of grace
in the administration of life.
How blessed we are
that You are more
   than what we make of You
that You do not fit
that You are so inconvenient
   so lacking in good form
   so impertinent to call.
O Fire in the ice
O Stillness in the stream
O Flowers filling out the sky
O Love beneath the ground
O Life within the tomb.

In songs and various forms of popular Christian spirituality, we refer to God as all-powerful or omnipotent. In general, our images of God's power arise more from the political experience of power in various periods of history.

During the classical and medieval periods, God's power was seen as similar to that of a king or a feudal lord. God was the sovereign power. The concept was slightly modified to include the image of God as a kind and good sovereign who exercised power not only as a judge but also as a merciful father.

This image of God's power was further modified by many of the more modern experiences of power that I have mentioned. God was imagined as the one who was all knowing, who could foresee the future and all needs in the present. God was provident and, essentially, in control.

This view of an omnipotent God who is in control of human beings and the universe has shaped religious attitudes regarding predestination. It was this controlling God who was so thoroughly rejected by the modern quest for human autonomy and freedom. It was this controlling God who had to be cut down to size, as it were, to make room for human freedom.

At the time of the Protestant Reformation, God became the sovereign not so much out there or up there but as the inward reality of the sovereign conscience. In what has been called "the turn to the subject," contemporary theologians have attempted to articulate an experience of God as the ground of human freedom and power rather than as a threat.

There are some rather unfortunate consequences to these various images of God's power. If God's power is seen as sovereign, it can be used to buttress various ideological views of empire. Our God must be the highest, just as we are the greatest power. If we imagine that our leaders are always right, just as God is always right, then we will be inclined toward an unquestioning attitude to authority, as happened in Germany during the Nazi era.

If God is imaged as being in control, then the problem of evil reemerges with a vengeance. If God is good and God is all-powerful, that is to say in control, then why is there evil in the world? Given the ambiguous ways in which we human beings have imagined the power of God, the ways that have suited our own purposes, some theologians have suggested that we strip from our concept of God all notions of power. Someone like Dietrich Bonhoeffer, who had seen God used to legitimate the Holocaust, cried out, "Only a suffering God can save us now."

However, to make God powerless would not only make God once again innocent, not responsible for the evil in the world, but it would also make God ineffectual, powerless to do good. We need to believe in a God who makes a difference in this world, who makes all the difference in the world.

Thus, I am led back to the God of beginnings who created the most fundamental relationships of power, in whose creative power the world was creation and each one of us a creature of God.

To acknowledge that we are creatures is not to say that God has all the power and we have none. God's power is not some great pie in the sky in which God will always have the biggest piece. It is to say that power exists when we are in relationship to God. It is to say that when we relate to the earth as God's creation, we share in the creative power of God.

To acknowledge that we are creatures is to say that we share in the creative power of God. When we are in relationship with God, there is energy for the good, which belongs neither to God nor to us but which happens when we interact. We must search for those conditions that help us sustain our relationship with God and ensure that this relationship is the source of creative power within a group. We need to find ways of living within relationships of creative power and this I would like to explore further in chapter six.

Our relationship with the Creator is the source of creative power, which is the power to begin something new, to begin as someone new. Sexuality has the potential to become either a destructive or a controlling form of power. It can also become the creative power of a new relationship, of two renewed and re-created people, and the creation of a new human being. Ultimately, the power of the One Who Creates is the power to create something or someone out of nothing—to raise from the dead. The One Who Creates is also the One Who Redeems.

A sense of gratitude and astonishment reawakens us to the mystery of creation and our own beginnings. It is this same attitude that reconnects us with the source of our power. Gratitude is the source of our power and the point of any exercise of creative power.

Nelson Mandela expressed it this way in his inaugural address as president of South Africa:

Our deepest fear is not that we are inadequate. Our deepest fear is that we are powerful beyond measure. It is our light not our darkness that frightens us. We ask ourselves, "Who am I to be brilliant, gorgeous, talented, fabulous?" Actually, who are you not to be? You are a child of God. Your playing small doesn't serve the world. There's nothing enlightened about shrinking so that other people won't feel insecure around you. We are born to manifest the glory of God that is within us. It's not just in some of us. It's in everyone, and, as we let our light shine, we unconsciously give other people permission to do the same. As we are liberated from our own fear, our presence automatically liberates others.

Real Powerlessness and Radical Powerlessness

I have explored how our imaginations are shaped by the forced alternatives of being totally in control or being totally powerless. I have also suggested that it would probably be more true to say that we have some real power, probably much more than we think or are willing to admit. Although we cannot do everything, this does not mean we can do nothing. We can do something and I believe there is at least one thing that each one of us is called to do in this life. This is what is meant by humility: to truthfully acknowledge what we can do.

The story is told of a little chick and a rabbit that were walking along the road. All of a sudden there was a bolt of thunder. The rabbit ran off along the road and began yelling, "The sky is falling. The sky is falling." He looked back only to see the little chick was lying on his back with his feet thrust up into the sky. The rabbit ran back and asked: "Little chick, the sky is falling! What are you doing?"

"One does what one can," replied the little chick.

Once we have overcome our false sense of powerlessness, we can assume some sense of power—which is limited but nonetheless real. We can begin to distinguish false powerlessness from the very real powerlessness that we do experience in some areas of our lives. In making such a distinction, we begin to have the wisdom to know where we can make changes and where we can't. We can also begin to distinguish between real powerlessness and a much more fundamental sense of powerlessness which I call radical powerlessness. When we leave behind the unnecessary illusions of powerlessness, we can enter more freely into the realm of radical powerlessness where we experience the power of God in a new way.

Our two most fundamental human experiences of radical powerlessness are in the mysterious events of birth and death, events over which we have no control. None of us can make ourselves be born. We are brought into this world through others and, although some would like to control the time and manner of their death, none of us can reverse the final outcome. We who take our own birth so for granted do not want to be surprised by death when it comes to us or to those whom we love.

It is when we reflect on the mystery of our birth and the certainty of our death that we are given the gracious opportunity to experience anew the power of God which is the power to create, to bring something or someone out of nothingness. I have reflected on the mystery of our beginnings in the previous chapter. It is my belief that if we could once again be astonished by the miracle of our own beginnings we would find it easier to believe that we, in the moment of death, when we are quite, quite nothing, could just as graciously be born again out of nothingness through the creative power of God. Such rebirth is a possibility every day. We can die before we die.

The Power of Jesus

You arise again
between us and among us
Power of Creation
Power of Salvation
Power of our power

Length of our eyes
Soundness in our ears
Calling in our mouths
Sureness in our steps
Concentration of our mind
Largeness of our heart.

In the gospels we read the story of someone who knew the mystery of creative power. Jesus continually proclaimed that he was *from* God, that he had his origin and beginning in God, that he was a child of God, a Son of God. This was why he called God "Father." We know that the word "Father" is as inadequate to describe the parental quality of God as is the word "Mother." Nevertheless, what Jesus was saying was that he had been born of God.

In the previous chapter I suggested that the birth of each person is so miraculous that we can say, over and above the fact that our parents had a great deal to do with this, that we are indeed children of God. In Jesus, we see the example of someone who lived his life totally and completely within this awareness. It was why his entire life was an act of gratitude. Again and again, he blessed God, offered thanksgiving. Living in a sense of radical gratitude, he gave his life away so freely and so generously that others were astonished by his actions.

Like God, Jesus looked on the world and saw that it was very good. He recognized the hunger and thirst for goodness that lie beneath every form of dissatisfaction. He came to free people from their false sense of guilt and to call them to repentance for those deeds of theirs that were consequential. Living in a sense of radical gratitude, he liberated people. In his teaching he presented a vision of what it would mean to live happily.

Because he knew he was *from God*, he also lived in the realization that he was *with God*, that his identity was constituted through this most fundamental relationship. This was the source of his power. The authority of Jesus was not something that he wielded like a stick but something that became real and alive because of his relationship to the One who had created him.

Thus, we see that the power of Jesus was not something which he claimed as a possession nor was it something which God gave to him as a donation. The power of Jesus was the energy that was activated through his relationship with God. Jesus did not hoard power and then dole it out as needed. In the act of his speaking, the power of God became audible. As he touched, the energy of God transformed those who were in need.

It was not a controlling power, not a power achieved by wealth, might, or position. It was the power of love unleashed through active gratitude.

Throughout history, Christians have tried to tame and control the power of Jesus. Institutionalized religion has all too often abandoned the summons to live in a sense of gratitude and in relationship with God as Jesus did. What is left may be authority, but without the power to heal and transform the world. What is left may be words, but without the power to persuade. The times when the church has appeared most controlling and domineering were the times of its weakest faith in the power of Jesus as real and active.

All too often Jesus is presented as the model of innocent powerlessness and it is true that he did not have power in a controlling sort of way. But this does not mean that he lacked power. This does not mean that he was only a victim or survivor.

Real victims are forced into suffering not of their choosing. This was not the case with Jesus. He chose to base his life on the way of gratitude and he chose all the consequences of that. In the end, it brought him into conflict with people who could not understand this form of power and wanted to bring it under control.

In the trial of Jesus we see two conflicting views of the way the world really works. Jesus had come to make the world a place in which it was a little easier to be grateful. Others wanted a world in which it would be possible to get more and to be more in control. For a time it seemed that the way of gratitude was as passing and vulnerable as the lilies of the field.

Along the way of the cross, Jesus met those who played their part as victims, oppressors, and bystanders. The power of his love broke through the cycle of captivity that held them all chained to their social roles. To the thieves who were about to die, he said: "You are more than victims, you are sons of God." To the soldiers who were about to kill him, he said: "You are more than oppressors—you have it in you to be good, to do good." Before Pilate who wielded power but acted as though he was a victim of circumstances beyond his control, Jesus stood silent. He did not wash his hands of Pilate.

There were many bystanders, then as now, who watched, who wondered, who were curious. They were invited to step out of their paralysis and to assume the burden of the cross.

It would be a mistake to think the story of the crucifixion glorifies the situation of the victim. In assuming the consequences of his life, and in the manner of his death, Jesus pointed the way to a world in which there would be no more victims, oppressors, or helpless bystanders. That crucifixion was meant to be the last, not the precursors of many others to follow.

Nailed to the cross, Jesus experienced radical powerlessness. In a moment of abandonment, "My God, my God, why have You forsaken me?", his relationship with God seemed broken. In this moment he was quite, quite nothing.

Yet in this moment of radical powerlessness he experienced once again the creative power of God—the power to create someone new out of nothingness...as in the beginning. This was a new beginning, resurrection.

For the early Christians, this new beginning was as astonishing as if on the first day of creation. Only this time it was called Salvation and Redemption.

The Power of Christian Community

> *Because money talks*
> *but rarely conceives*
> *Because money talks*
> *but does not walk*

We call upon Your name
because there are things
money can't buy
because what does it profit us
if we consume the whole world
and are consumed in the process
because we are tired
of being paralyzed
in pain and guilt and powerlessness.

We call upon Your name
when we have neither silver nor gold
or when we have it all
and it means nothing.
We call upon the Power
of Your name, Your Power
between us and among us.
Like Peter we say
to ourselves, sick and lame
by the gate—
Rise. Walk.
Sing Justice. Sow Glory.

After the death of Jesus, some of the disciples were tempted to return to their familiar worlds of captivity. Having betrayed each other and having felt that their dreams and hopes were lost, they wandered along the road to Emmaus, the small town where they could live with a modest sense of futility. Yet, these people, who were going nowhere, whose relationships had become self-defeating, were transformed by the memory and unseen presence of Jesus. A group of weak and powerless people was turned once again toward hope. They gathered in what was called the Upper Room for a very long time. I imagine that this was a time of intense interaction, of talking, of eating together and praying together. It may even have been a time of intense discussion and debate. They surely recalled all of the events that had happened and what Jesus had taught in the way he lived and the way he died.

In other words, they grew in relation to one another and in relationship with Jesus. As this happened, power grew among them and between them until it could only be imagined as the flames of fire of Pentecost.

From there they went forth in great power. The writings of the early Christians are filled with descriptions of this power. In a sense, it became a self-fulfilling prophecy. Convinced now of the creative power of God, they went forth and preached forgiveness, grace, and gratitude. They had no money to offer those who asked for help, but they offered instead a word of power: Arise. Walk.

They began to live differently, to strengthen one another so that it was possible to live gratefully even in the midst of a great and powerful empire.

And indeed, this little group of people did transform the world.

For those of us who weaken at the thought of ever being set free from the chains of consumerism that bind us, the memory of this little group offers some important lessons.

- We experience power by being in relationship with God.

- We experience power when "two or three" are gathered in his name.

- This kind of power has everything to do with the quality of relationship and with the possibility of sustained interaction.

- Prayer is the sustained interaction with God that provides the condition for participating in the power of God.

- A prayerful community of faith provides the condition for sustained interaction between persons and God.

The first Christians were energized by the conviction that the power of Jesus had the potential to transform the world, almost overnight. That was not to be. The power of empire threatened to crush this movement of hope and eventually even attempted to co-opt it. During this period of history Christians struggled more deeply to understand what Jesus had come *for*. His passionate energy was connected to a power that had a point and a purpose. He knew he had come from God and was with God in power, but he was also for God as the point of his being. The question of the meaning and purpose of life was one that was as important to the early Christians as it is to us here and now in America, the North and the West—in a time of endings and beginnings.

———————

You arise again
between us and among us
within us and beyond us
Love without end
breaking out
from the tombs of our times
the containers of our lives.
Even death could not contain You.
Power to begin again
Power to create anew
Power to lift us up
and draw us on
Power of our power.

CHAPTER FIVE

The Point of Our Being

You are the Point
of all Being.
Every tree stretches
up to You.
Each plant reaches
down to You.
All the roads go
on to You.
The many waters run
toward the vastness
of Your love.
The air breathes
in and unto You.
Every heart wants
to turn to You.
How unhappy we are
when we miss
the Point of all Being.
How blessed are we
when we follow our longing
and leaning into
Your direction.

Here in America, the North and the West, it is easy to miss the point of it all. There are so many points to be made, goals to be achieved. We move from point to point and from scene to scene. One point disappears as another surfaces just beyond our reach. The point shifts, moves, and changes direction.

There are no compasses here or at least none that seem obvious. The point of it all seems to be getting more points. This is how it seems when we miss the original point of our being.

She gets up and turns on the television to find out what is happening...

He turns around and sees someone coming up the steps behind him, so he takes them two at a time and then three at a time and there is no landing in sight...

She kissed him and then kissed him again because it was the first time or was it the second or third time since the last time...

He was wallpapering the living room for the seventh time in the seventh house since they had been together and had begun to renovate their lives...

Leaving sentences in mid-air, they moved in and out of groups at the wine and cheese party, lured by fragments of new information...

Since there wasn't any deadline, they weren't sure when to get out of bed—or why.

Episodic Meaning

These are scenes from lives lived in episodes. These are not the anguished lives described by European existentialists who had concluded that life was absurd and meaningless. These are the lives of good and hard-working Americans who do have experiences of meaning, but there is little or no connection between one episode and the next.

Our lives are starting to resemble a television series. Episode by episode, the series "grabs" the viewers. We are familiar with the characters and the situation within which they play out their lives. Yet, the series is so constructed that we can tune into only one episode and find it meaningful, we can miss many episodes and still find it possible to get the "drift" of it. There is no underlying narrative to the television series, just as there is no underlying story to give meaning to our lives. So people tune in and tune out.

We cannot find the story line, the narrative structure that strings together all the various episodes of our lives. There seem to be no beginning, no turning points or end, no conclusion. It becomes difficult to identify high points and low points, which ones matter and which ones don't. Our politicians do not lie in the good old-fashioned way. They are sincerely telling the truth at the moment, even if it contradicts a truth that they just as sincerely told in another moment.

A culture that lives on episodic meanings is one in which it becomes ever more difficult to lead consequential lives. If there is no connection between the episodes of our lives, why should it matter what we do and how we live? Episodes of meaning do not add up to direction or purpose and they may even intensify our sense of meaninglessness and powerlessness.

Even our sincerest efforts to create some space for a healthier lifestyle or time for spirituality may become yet more episodes in a life that we do not see or experience as whole. We may alternate between gratitude and ingratitude in yet another episodic way.

Consider date books, their shape and size and color, how they are used and why. Not only are they helpful, they are also a sign of identity and maybe even purpose in life. You can tell a person, so they say, by his or her date book. The fuller it is the more important you must be, the more meaningful your life—or so it would seem. You sense your true insignificance when someone merely pencils you in—and tilts the date book toward you so you can see how lucky you are to have been fitted in between all those other to do's. An empty day in a date book can seem like a day devoid of meaning and purpose. No crisis seems worse than losing your date book, because then you wouldn't know what you were supposed to do or when.

Yet, would you still know why? That is the question. Is there any thread of meaning, any sense of direction and purpose that flows through all those pages of a date book? Are the pages of our days held together by anything more than a cover?

These are hard questions to ask. However, it is my belief that they are also hopeful questions, because we could not even begin to ask such questions were there not already within us some intimations of an answer.

Lifelines from the Past

In the past, the underlying narrative structure of our lives was supplied by our culture, by our country, or by religion, sometimes even by sports. The modern myth of progress carried our lives forward by the sheer force of its optimism ever since the founding of America. The American spirit was essentially expansive and, at its best, extremely generous. The founding vision of the republic and the ideals of life, liberty, and the pursuit of happiness carried the nation forward as it grew. The mainline religions preached a biblical story that revealed the origin and the destiny of the human person.

These lifelines still exist, but they no longer seem strong enough to pull us out of the cultural currents of consumerism. The events of the twentieth century, simultaneously barbaric and eminently modern, have raised doubts about the myth of progress in a way that no philosophical critique could do. The founding ideals of the republic are becoming lost in the imperatives of empire. To the extent that the mainline religions tied their message to the dominant myths of the culture, their voices too have become uncertain and lost.

What we are left with are fragmentary and often colliding insights, isolated achievements, and singular moments of glory and generosity. Michael Ondaatje describes this situation brilliantly in his book, *The English Patient.* "So the books for the Englishman, as he listened intently or not, had gaps of plot like sections of a road washed out by storms."

Determining which one of those pieces will matter at any given time now seems to be only a matter of personal preference or political power. In politics, as in religion, single issues become the only way of responding to the welter of daily events.

Within various church communities, we find ourselves similarly fragmented. Only a few Catholics, for example, would pretend that we are still guided by a single and integrated vision of life and the world. We are sustained by fragments of a tradition, beautiful fragments, true fragments. But there often seems to be no whole greater than these great parts. Most Catholics return to Mass on Christmas Eve and rejoice in the sense of mystery that is communicated through the sacraments. But they no longer sense the whole world as breathing with some mysterious significance. The day after Christmas, McDonald's is McDonald's; a hamburger is a hamburger and the more the better. Religion is for certain times and places, here and there, more or less—and always in moderation.

In the following pages, I want to reflect on how some of these lifelines have now become ties that bind us and hold us captive in new and different ways. It will involve considerations of the collapse of larger systems of meaning, but such considerations are not merely theoretical. The consequences of such a crisis are, as always, deeply and personally experienced.

A simple yet sure sign of the loss of spirit and meaning is fatigue. When I reflect on the times I have worked because I believed in what I was doing and had a conviction about its purpose, I realize that I could work for hours and wake refreshed. It is when I was not convinced of the purpose of what I was doing that I became easily tired, took long breaks, began to plan holidays, took courses on how to manage my time and on how to set boundaries.

I recall a conversation with a friend of mine who was fretting about caring for her young son. She is very busy, as is her husband. They get up, get the child ready for day care, go to work, come home, make supper, get the child ready for bed, prepare for work the next day. "Sometimes I feel my life is just a collection of pieces," she said. The conversation would have been usual enough except for the fact that she went on to say: "But what I love to do, later in the evening before I go to bed, is to go into my son's room and just look at him. I just love looking at him. And then all the fatigue falls away and I know the point of it all."

The point of our lives concentrates all that we are and all that we do and fills us with the energy of purpose. That point becomes the line that gathers unto itself all the other points of our lives. This may not mean our lives are progressing or even getting better, but it does mean that we know why we are here and what we are for.

The Myth of Progress

The storyline called progress has shaped America more than any place else on earth. Even Christians who supposedly lived by another storyline internalized this myth so deeply that it became difficult for them to separate optimism from hope. The belief in the myth of progress gave us a way of understanding our lives, a narrative to live by. What is the point of your life? To better yourself, to make a better world.

The value of a better life seemed so obvious that few questioned it or the consequences of such an attitude. As a purpose in life, it seemed almost self-evident. The most important question then became *how*, how to get a better life. In our day-to-day lives we internalized this worldview rather deeply as the conviction that if we just worked hard enough and thought smart enough then things would get better and better. Know-how and can-do.

Many things did get better. Children were inoculated, education became more accessible and human rights were respected in new and important ways. All the while, the questions of "how" consumed us. Our bookstores are now full of "how to" books for every imaginable task: how to teach, how to live simply, how to make love, how to pray, how to cook, how to make friends and influence people, how to win without really trying. We have become specialists in the hows of life but we hardly know why anymore.

There is a shadow side to the energetic and expansive drive toward personal and social progress. At its root, the myth of progress is built on a radical dissatisfaction with the past and the present. As such, it undercuts any attitude of fundamental gratitude. Just as the modern myth of autonomy stifles the radical amazement of gratitude and as the modern reliance on controlling knowledge undercuts a creative sense of power, so too the modern notion of progress consumes a sense of meaning and purpose.

Within this myth, the future becomes the primary tense: the past is something that has already become obsolete, or at least quaint, and the present is already being consumed on the way to the future. For the sake of a better future, people will save, sacrifice, and work—very hard.

Strange bedfellows on the left and right of the political spectrum have shared this conviction. Such a worldview buttressed a lot of positive thinking, sometimes called hope.

Parents expected that their children would be better off than they were. People involved in social change felt there was reason to believe that things would get better if they just worked hard enough and smart enough. Church groups felt that there was no problem so big (loss of numbers, loss of revenue) that it could not be overcome with the right kind of program and strategy. Consultants became the new high priests who specialized in the "how to" of doing things better and better.

Yet, we now have reason to wonder whether all our knowledge and technology have made the world a better place. The doubt that gripped another generation as it fought for useless yards of territory during the First World War, that surfaced anew after Auschwitz and Hiroshima, has now become widespread. If this is what technology can do, can we trust it? Can we still believe in progress when barbarism has worn such a civilized face?

As the twenty-first century unfolds even further, many more people are beginning to fear the effects of technology. Environmentalists are waving the red flag, signaling the extent to which technology is destroying the biosphere. Many are afraid of what biotechnicians and genetic engineers are concocting in their test tubes. The question of the limits of growth has now become part of everyday discussions.

In the new global economic order, many people are no longer so sure that tomorrow will be better. Young people know that working hard and thinking smart does not necessarily guarantee a better tomorrow. After September 11, any easy optimism in the future has been shattered and the sense of insecurity has deepened.

We are only beginning to realize the enormous crisis of spirit that accompanies such doubts about the future. Some religious people may clap their hands with glee as the great modern secular myths begin to disintegrate. They do so at their own peril. To the extent that many good religious people have internalized the optimistic view of the future that has floated easily through the air of this culture, then they too will be shaken in the depths of their being when things do not seem to be getting better.

What do church congregations do when they have worked very hard and thought very smart and things don't get better? Numbers decline, contributions are down in spite of enormous efforts. It becomes less easy to hope, because our illusions have been nourished for so long by cultural optimism. How difficult it is for all of us, believers and non-believers alike, to say those words that amount to a sort of cultural heresy: *It's not working anymore. We've thought hard and worked smart and it's not working. We don't know what to do.* Such an admission may indeed be a crisis, but it is also a moment for the birth of authentic faith and hope when, out of the nothingness of not knowing, something or someone new may be created.

The myth of progress not only generated optimism but it also created nostalgia—a longing for the past, not as it was but as a better version of the present. Both optimism and nostalgia lead to a disparagement of the present, either as less than what could have happened or as an inferior version of what has happened. Thus, throughout American popular culture we have nostalgic memories of Pleasantville, of places where Father Knows Best, of little towns that bear no resemblance to the ugly big cities of today.

Interestingly enough, in a culture that tends to view whatever happened in the social and historical past as somehow inferior, the past has reasserted itself as a basic dogma of much of contemporary psychology. Unlocking the secrets of the past is seen as the key to personal liberation.

In sum, the myth of progress has consumed the real present and the real past on the way to some better future. It has been fuelled by an all-consuming dissatisfaction with the past and the present. Gratitude can be only a future possibility.

From Better to More

One would think that a secular myth that has so shaped the lives of North Americans would have been thoroughly discredited by the realities of life in the twentieth century. Nevertheless, it has persisted, albeit in a transformed version in the most thoroughgoing form of materialism. If one can no longer believe that things will get *better and better*, then maybe it is still be possible to believe that there can be *more and more* for *more and more* people—if we just work hard enough and think smart enough. Thus, consumerism has become the materialistic contortion of the modern secular version of meaning. Consumer confidence has become the new economic indicator of hope. Optimism is now tied to the rise and fall of the market.

In the imperative of *more*, the economically generated dissatisfaction of consumerism is combined with the inherent dissatisfaction of the myth of progress in a potent mix. Is it any wonder that we find it difficult to be grateful in a more than intermittent way?

The way in which consumerism obscures the loss of meaning in the modern myth is powerfully illustrated in Picasso's painting

"The Charnel House," which was conceived at the end of World War II. In the upper left-hand corner is a comfortable still-life composition of a pitcher and casserole atop a small table. Underneath are corpses ravaged by hunger and neglect, strung in astonished death, the unquiet dead of modern, total war. As art critic John Bentley Mays reflects:

> The great art of our time, I believe, will be an art of this paradox and absurdity, of luxury and the quiet horror hidden under the table. Such is our legacy from the 20th century, and our unique destiny; to have our pleasures, to create, to live out our days here in the peaceable kitchen of capitalist prosperity—to feast and banter and enjoy ourselves round the table beneath which lie the rotting corpses, the heaps of memories, of the modern centuries' innocent dead.

Where once the vision of modernity was a vast and grand view of history without end, it has now become merely the unending process of consumption, the consumption of everything including time itself. It is a situation in which the past and the present are robbed of meaning and the future also ceases to exist as an ideal or hope because it will surely be tossed off as soon as it is attained. What is the point of it all? More. Tomorrow and tomorrow does not a future make.

The Empire of More

The Decline of the American Empire is the name of an award-winning film by director Denys Arcand. In the opening scene, we hear an articulate and rather jaded academic analyze the present state of affairs for a young radio interviewer. In a time of political decline, says the professor, people cease to invest their energy in a common social project and turn toward more personal projects, such as the development and fulfillment of the self. Only in developing societies, she lectures, is there a common social vision compelling enough to invite individuals to transcend their personal interests for the sake of something greater.

The rest of this film is an exploration of the cultivation of the self, which takes place as a group of Montreal academics goes on a weekend together. The women exercise on Nautilus equipment while the men cook a gourmet meal. Commitments of every kind fall by the wayside on this weekend—all for the sake of more personal pleasure or power, power in the mode of domination. What remains is only a vague sense of belonging to a group which could dissolve at any moment.

One curious statement floats out unexpectedly near the end of the film: "We have no vision, no models or metaphors to live by. Only the saints and mystics live well at a time like this."

The words echo those spoken during the time of the Babylonian captivity: "We have in our day no priest, no prophet, no leader or king. We do not even have the words with which to offer sacrifice" (Dn 3:38).

This film is an example of the way artists often name the reality of a culture before they or we know it in any conceptual or analytic form. Between the facts of our social experience and any reflection on them, we need the mediating images of artists and storytellers to give us some way of reading the signs of the times.

Whether we know it or not, those of us who live in the Western world are going through a massive shift in historical consciousness: from a consciousness of being part of a well-developed world to an inchoate awareness of being part of a declining culture. Some speak broadly of this as the "decline of the West" or "the decline of modernity." It is important to note here that no other nation has been so shaped by the ideals of modernity as has the United States. As England used to be the center of Western civilization in the nineteenth century, so in the twentieth century America became the center around which nations have circled with only relative degrees of power and independence. It has not been inaccurate to say that as America goes, so goes the West. This is why, throughout this book, I have used America, the North and the West to describe not only a geographical reality but also a state of mind.

Even in the aftermath of September 11, America still seems relatively powerful and in control. Indeed, it would seem to be the only superpower on earth and the country with the greatest wealth and military might. Yet, can we still argue that it is a nation, an empire that has a strong coherent sense of the common good which summons loyalty and sacrifice? We can summon the will to fight against an enemy, but is there an equal willingness to sacrifice for the common good? Governments find it increasingly difficult to ask their citizens to pay taxes that will strengthen the fabric of society. We may have gained the whole world only to suffer the loss of our own soul.

It is not easy to entertain the thought that we are living in an "empire." The word conjures up images of exploitation, which seem to conflict with our stated political values of freedom, justice, and tolerance.

The transition from a small republic to a world empire took place at the end of the Second World War. An empire was born to save the nation and the globe itself from communism. The explosion of a nuclear bomb by Russia in 1951 was the definitive beginning of the Cold War, a forty-year period of history that would enlist much of the economic, political, and spiritual energy of America.

For all of us who live in the heart of empire or in one of its colonies, it is uncomfortable to think of ourselves as living in a time of historical decline. We see ourselves as living in a "developed" world and tend to refer to other countries to the south as being part of the "underdeveloped world." What a sea change it would be for us to begin to think of ourselves as part of an overdeveloped or even a declining empire.

The decline cannot be defined primarily in economic terms, at least not at the moment. Nevertheless, to the extent that America has tied its future to the global marketplace it has become increasingly vulnerable to the wide swings of the stock market. We are rapidly moving to a multipolar world where there are not one but many centers of economic activity. In the United States, as in all countries throughout the Western world, the process of globalization is seriously shaking the political form of the nation-state. America as an economy and as a lifestyle now knows no bounds and encompasses the world, but that world is also erasing the boundaries of what was once called the United States. The monied classes of various countries now have more in common with each other than they do with the poor and disenfranchised of the underworld of the culture of money.

Canada is a colony of this empire. It has always been a colony of some empire: first of the French, then of the British, and now of the United States. The free trade deal with America and all of the consequences of that agreement have firmly established our colonial identity. Thus Canadians, as Northrop Frye has said, "know that the head office is someplace else."

All of us, in America, the North and the West, have been part of a great empire. We have shared in the benefits of its surging growth and we are now slightly bewildered by its apparent vulnerability. Nevertheless, the possibility of a lesser greatness may also summon us to think about new political and economic forms of goodness—of smaller forms of the common good, of lighter visions.

Without a Vision the People Perish

I am reluctant to read history according to some organized model that assumes that every new political experiment, like every seed in the ground, is doomed to mature, age, and die. This view of history denies the not insignificant factor of human choice and action, which can change the course of history. Nevertheless, there are historic trends, which, at some point, cannot be reversed except by some quantum leap of the imagination. At these moments, historical breakdowns can become historical breakthroughs.

There are lessons from history that may be too pertinent to ignore. Rome was once also a small republic that thrived as its citizens participated in the political process and as the people of the conquered colonies were granted citizenship and status. Gradually the empire grew and, as the need to control the colonies became more demanding, a whole military-industrial complex developed. Soon the empire consumed the vision of the republic.

Rome grew in wealth, but the vision of a more decent way of life declined. Hedonism reigned. Sports became a means of entertainment and escape. The religions of state and various cults thrived. The senators came to represent not the good of the republic but rather the needs of special interest groups. Citizens no longer fought for their country but hired mercenaries instead to make the sacrifice.

The Decline of the American Empire focuses on the difference between living in a society in a state of development and merely existing in a culture in a state of decline. The difference, so the film suggests, has to do with the relative strength or weakness of the common social vision within which an individual lives.

Every social movement or political experiment begins with a vision that animates it and draws it forward. The vision may be stated in the most poetically intuitive images or it may be articulated in a politically refined constitution. In either case, the vision compels the response of those who share in it. A common social vision or ideal is something people aspire to, are exhilarated by, and are willing to make sacrifices for. It transforms present action and interprets it in terms of future possibilities.

The fading of that vision coincides with the dissolution, whether sudden or gradual, of the social movement or socio-political institutions in which it is embodied. The historical precedent of the Roman Empire is once again pertinent here. Scholars have identified several possible causes of the breakdown of this empire (which took place over several hundred years), and the debate continues as to which of these causes was the key factor. However, this much seems clear: The empire's economic and political collapse coincided with the slow disintegration of the architectonic vision upon which it was built.

Here and now, "the economy" is running the government and its social and foreign policy rather than the other way around. The foreign policy of America is now conducted primarily on the basis of what is best for trade, for generating more trade. Because of these interests, America will support dictatorships and abandon issues of human rights. And it will sometimes use hired mercenaries, called U.N. peacekeepers, to do the task. The needs of the economy do not demand democracy but they do demand a stable world order. The economy demands a military-industrial complex even if it is at the expense of some stated ideals such as open and public debate and the right of citizens to have a say in the policies of their government.

Sports, which were often a deeply felt exercise in loyalty and identity, have also been transformed by the dynamics of empire. Players move around frequently from team to team, sold to the highest bidder. Fans can no longer feel the same loyalty to the players, who are simply doing a job for the moment. Sports may have become spectacles, but they no longer provide heroes or myths to live by.

Citizens have become consumers. They are invested more in the success of corporations than in the bonds of their own governments. They believe there is more money to be made in speculating on money than in investing in the real work of real businesses. We get the governments we deserve and if most of us would prefer *more* rather than a meaningful way of life, then governments will not lead where the people will not follow.

Without a compelling social vision of the future, a commonweal, we may choose to live in the past as we imagine it to have been (nostalgia) or to live for the present moment. "Eat, drink, and be merry for tomorrow you may perish." Then there are those for whom the diminished sense of a social future becomes associated with the end of the whole world. This apocalyptic view is held by groups as diverse as religious fundamentalists, Y2K-type survivalists, and certain environmental groups. Apocalyptic thinking leads some groups to less social involvement and others to more political action.

Some of the developments within the New Age movement are indicative of a tendency to flee history entirely when faced with a fading sense of the future. As the external world appears more fragile, there is a cultivation of interiority, or subjectivity, in an effort to reach a "consciousness" that transcends the vicissitudes of a particular time and place.

The return to the processes of nature and the self has always been characteristic of those periods in history when political and social processes are breaking down. "Consciousness" becomes the way to connect with nature and the self outside of the forced march or retreat of history. The turn toward interiority and subjectivity has always been characteristic of periods of historical decline in which individuals have felt less confident about shaping the external world.

This loss of a sense of the future, which is so characteristic of North America at this time, has a bearing on many of today's seemingly disparate social issues. Only a very present-centered society, for example, will lay waste the environment and leave it as a garbage heap for future generations. Only such a society will risk a global holocaust in order to preserve its present way of life. There is a dangerous myopia in mortgaging the future through spending policies in which the benefit to a few now will be paid for by many in the years to come. The contentious question of abortion is another example of an issue that has been cast in mainly present-centered terms. Often abortion is disputed in terms of the rights of women versus the rights of the unborn. Given the past history of patriarchy, in society and in the churches, it is inevitable that there will be those who claim that seeing abortion as an issue of women's rights is an advance. Nevertheless, when we consider (and this is admittedly a gross and partial consideration) that at least half of the unborn are future or potential women, it becomes more difficult to cast abortion simply as an issue of women's rights. It is perhaps more accurate to say that it is an issue of whether the rights and needs of the women and men of this generation will take precedence over the right of the women and men of future generations to take their place in this world.

Political Ways of Coping with a Loss of Vision

The effort to cope with the loss of an overarching social vision and an imperative sense of the future takes at least two significant forms within North America today. To use familiar terms, they can be called the "conservative" and the "liberal" options. Obviously, my description of either of these options must necessarily remain sketchy, since neither conservatism nor liberalism exists as some ideal and unchanging type. Their particular character is modified by many regional and national differences and by the issues that have characterized various periods in North American political history. The conservative tradition in Canada, for example, is quite different from the conservative tradition in the United States. Liberalism tends to be considered more middle of the road in Canada than in the United States.

Nevertheless, certain characteristics of each of these political options can and should be noted. My purpose in sketching the outlines of these two political options is to suggest how both of them are ways of coping with a loss of common social vision. These tendencies can also exist within each of us and can lead to rather different forms of spirituality.

The conservative effort (on the part of many and diverse groups) is directed toward bringing back some order and meaning in society. Quite simply, conservatives are concerned about the chaos and confusion they perceive in the lives of individuals and society. This concern is freshly evident in the members of the new information class who must be constantly flexible because of the fluid nature of their work. The need for something more stable and enduring becomes an almost necessary counterbalance to their work. Thus, the concern about family, morality, and traditional values. The forces of the New Right seem to have a very clear vision of America and its place in the world and they often articulate that vision in economic terms and in the language of religion. I remember a well-known Republican politician telling me that he believed that "Capitalism is God's greatest gift to the world."

Although I do not agree with many of the solutions the New Right has for the problems in our society, I do sense that they may well be closer to the heart of the problem than many give them credit for. They have tapped into a deep and legitimate need for a sense of direction and meaning and for commonly held values in public life.

However, it would seem that the conservative effort is doomed to fail for at least two significant social reasons. The first has to do with the internal contradiction between social conservatism (the value of the family, etc.) and economic conservatism. It is difficult to argue that laws should govern personal morality and, at the same time, to insist on a laissez-faire attitude toward the conduct of the marketplace. The social consequences of the free-market system are disastrous for traditional social institutions such as the family and religion. The demands of the market have closed down small family businesses (Mom and Pop stores) and forced people to move away from their extended families and their roots in communities of faith.

The second reason why the conservative effort, in the long run, is doomed to collapse is that a common social meaning and vision cannot be coerced, cannot be imposed. This is particularly true in a democratic society in which such an imposition would corrode the very basis upon which the nation was built. The conservative attempt to impose a common social vision, and thereby bring order into society, will almost always have to rely on the coercive, rather than the creative, use of power. The coercive use of power is characteristic of an empire in the state of decline. Ultimately, the conservative way of coping with social decline blinds its adherents to the extent to which they are subtly perpetuating the patterns of decline even as they attempt to come to grips with its disintegrating effects.

Liberalism is based on a philosophy that flowered in the nineteenth century and served to articulate the "beliefs" of the emerging economic order of industrial capitalism. Liberalism saw the free market as an interaction of conflicting individual interests that would eventually produce the greatest good for the greatest number of people. Liberalism did not then, and does not now, begin with an integrating vision of the whole but rather with the assumption that the individual is the starting point in economic, political, and social arrangements. Liberalism believes that the common good will result from the self-actualization of each part.

Liberal economics is based on a belief in an "invisible hand" that guides the competition between the various interests in the free market—for the benefit of all. In political terms, liberalism endorses the belief that the good of all is enhanced when each group pursues its own interests. It is inherently sympathetic to pluralism and stresses the social virtues of tolerance and individual rights. Culturally, liberals tend to believe that the more individuals have the freedom to express their thoughts and feelings, the greater will be the benefit to society as a whole.

The contributions of liberalism to Western civilization are many. Its emphasis on freedom of conscience and the tolerance necessary in a pluralistic society can be fully appreciated only when we think of the various forms of authoritarianism that preceded it. Yet, however much we may value this liberal tradition (politically, economically, and socially) we must face the fact that it has reached its limits.

This is most obviously true in the area of the economy. Liberalism works as long as the economic pie keeps expanding enough to sustain the belief that there will eventually be more for everyone. It assumes economic growth; neoliberal economics will always generate an over-heated economy. It flounders in a time of economic scarcity, when the economic pie begins to shrink. What happens when, for whatever reason, economic growth seems less possible? The serious fluctuations in the stock market suggest that there is no such thing as unlimited economic growth.

Liberalism cannot deal with the reality of limits. Once the size of the economic pie stops growing or begins to shrink, liberals are faced with the necessity of making choices between the benefits to some at the cost to others. As the necessity of establishing social policy and priorities becomes more obvious, liberalism seems even more ill equipped to respond to the challenge. Bereft of any common social vision, liberals search for some basis upon which to make decisions about social priorities. Without a common social vision, there is little basis for appealing to anything beyond self-interest. Witness the constant consultation of the polls in an effort to find some basis for deciding what would result in the greatest good for the greatest number of people.

All of this leads us to consider the most serious limitation of liberalism: its intrinsic inability to respond to the very deep human need for a common meaning and vision. People cannot live by freedom and tolerance alone. There is no salvation in interaction. Pluralism without purpose leads only to a labyrinth of processes and procedures.

The crisis of liberalism is ultimately a crisis of meaning.

A few significant words are noticeably absent from the liberal vocabulary today, words like sacrifice and commitment. Without a shared sense of vision, who can dare ask another to sacrifice certain things or indeed one's very self?

Liberals and conservatives are alike in that their patterns of coping with the decline of the empire mirror within themselves the patterns of that declining empire. As a result, they can offer no hope, no alternative for the future.

The Future and Class Time

The slipping away of the future as a common social faith affects people differently and the difference is often defined by their socio-economic status.

The rich and very powerful are still able to sustain the illusion that they can control the future. Those who are powerless and poor experience the future as just something that happens to you.

I remember being shocked when I heard that a young Guatemalan woman who had been living with us had suddenly begun to pack her bags even though she had only been with us for three months. When I asked her why she was leaving, she replied that three months had passed and so it must be time to leave because she had never stayed anywhere more than three months. When I asked her to stay, she started to cry. "No one ever asked me to stay before."

However, it is the middle class that has, less obviously but equally profoundly, been shaped by the imperative of the future. These are the people who plan for the future; they know what mortgages mean and they worry about the consequences of accumulated national debt and garbage. The middle class is also, therefore, the class that is most in crisis as that sense of future is being transformed in the culture of more. It is a painful crisis, but one that seems difficult to articulate and to take seriously.

What is the pain of the middle class? To probe the depths of this question, I begin with the assumption that people are defined interiorly as middle class not so much by a certain income or level of taxation but by the process of becoming part of that class.

Becoming qualified for jobs such as teaching, medicine, law, consulting, and social services involves a great deal of discipline. Fundamentally, it involves delaying gratification, making sacrifices now for some future benefits. Unlike those who inherit wealth or who are born into generations of poverty, people join the middle class only through effort and stay there only through effort. A middle-class status cannot be inherited or passed on. It is up to each individual to earn his or her way into this class. In sum, this is a class of people defined by discipline and formed through delayed gratification. This is a class of people forged through a sense of the future, people who have made sacrifices because there is a point to it all.

Until rather recently, these sacrifices made sense not only because there would be economic security in the end but also, and maybe even more important, because there would be definite satisfactions in one's work. For example, you could take satisfaction in knowing that you were making a difference, that you had a measure of power and control over your work. In a classroom, teachers had a great deal of freedom and responsibility. So did doctors and nurses within their areas of expertise. These were professionals, not employees. There was a point to their sacrifice.

Yet, gradually, this purpose changed. Some people were willing to exchange the satisfaction of their work for more money in less satisfying jobs. Then dissatisfactions set in and some were not willing to delay gratification any longer.

This advertisement says it all: *I'm just a good friend to myself, and I like to do what makes me feel good. Me, myself, and I used to sit around, putting things off until tomorrow. Tomorrow we'll buy new ski equipment and look at new compact cars. And pick up that new camera. The only trouble is that tomorrow always turned into the new tomorrow. And I never had a good time today. But now I live my dreams today, not tomorrow.*

As the search for better became the craving for more, middle-class people experienced a profound conflict between the sense of discipline and sacrifice that they had internalized and the desire for immediate gratification. Many who had sought a life found a lifestyle instead.

The more they became conspicuous consumers as exemplified in the style of the Yuppie—Perrier water, quiche, travel, the natural look—the more they searched for new forms of discipline.

Certain fears arise from individual self-definition through discipline—fear of going soft, fear of becoming undisciplined and flabby, fear of becoming obsolete as new technologies make previous learning antiquated. The middle class tends to scorn the apparent idleness of the poor and is suspicious of the decadence of the very rich. Softness appears fatal to those who are striving. There is a tendency to idealize "hard" times such as the Depression or war. The increasing preoccupation with diet and fitness is, perhaps, symbolic of a concern about moral flabbiness.

Health foods have grown in popularity; the concern with overeating seems to represent something more than simply worry about obesity. Where previous generations had been preoccupied with discipline and purity in sexual matters, now middle-class people have become more preoccupied with discipline and purity in matters of food. Catholics, who long ago had stopped eating fish instead of meat on Friday, embraced demanding regimes of diet and exercise.

The same kind of concern led to a certain middle-class discovery of the working class. Those who were concerned about the loss of traditional values and the increase of permissiveness viewed the working class as the embodiment of those values. So began the neo-conservative alliance between the working class and the neo-conservatives.

Not only exercise and diet but work itself became a kind of regenerating discipline, its own form of redemptive suffering. The discipline of work became the only source of moral regeneration, a regeneration that depended not on ethical options or spiritual conversion but on work itself.

All of this somehow reveals the dilemma of the middle class, which is caught between a sense of self fashioned through disciplined effort and a sense of self produced through the consumption of goods and experiences.

Imperial Ideologies

There are certain ideologies that assume the status of reality within an empire that sees itself as the center of the world. The ideologies of empire are expressed in psychologies and spiritualities of ME, HERE, and NOW.

Self-centeredness, self-preoccupation, self-preservation. These familiar dynamics haunt many families and places of work, many church groups and efforts at social justice. The destruction is everywhere to be seen. It is difficult to summon forth the sacrifice and self-forgetfulness that are essential for any common project, for any life held in common, for any common good in political and social life. In personal relationships as well as in political arrangements, self-interest is the operative ethic.

I once heard a very wise psychologist say that the psychological syndrome that is the most difficult to change is narcissism. He pointed out that almost every psychological approach only seems to accentuate a person's self-preoccupation.

My own sense is that the preoccupation with the self has deep roots in our socio-cultural context. It manifests itself in various psychological problems and in the crisis of many traditional religious values.

Is it any wonder that self-preoccupation should be so prevalent within a culture built on the assumption that it is the center of the world, the point of reference for the rest of the world?

Those who know they are at the social and political center of the world are more likely to treat "me" as an ultimate point of reference and "here" as the perspective from which to judge all other contexts. Within a great empire, it is easy to assume that this is "where it's at" and it seems almost natural to treat the now, the present, as the privileged point in time. This perspective can also be found even among socially conscious Americans who no longer see their country as the source of all good in the world but now see it as the cause of much of the evil in the world.

The NOW of course is not a real present but only the fleeting moment, which absorbs the past unto itself and consumes the future. The now is not the patient present, not the now that comes from being truly mindful, but a vortex that draws all unto itself.

Here are some of the maxims of an imperial psychology and spirituality: "Honor yourself." "You are the author of your own story." "Be true to your own process." "You are the most important project you will ever have."

It is as if the point of one's life is the maintenance and refurbishing of oneself. It is a project that will always degenerate into dissatisfaction.

The greedy, grasping, and even guilty self that sees itself as the center of the world can never be a grateful person, for a grateful person essentially knows where he or she is coming from and dwells in the present with a measure of awe. Essentially isolated and connected in only the vaguest way, the ungrateful remain with the illusion that they can exert some measure of control, if not over the world, then over themselves.

Thus, different political groups and different classes of people have ways of responding to the overall loss of a sense of the meaning and purpose of a culture. Getting more, being more is not enough to become the point of one's life.

The loss of a common sense of purpose experienced in personal and political ways has some dangerous consequences.

When the sense of meaning and purpose in a culture is weakened, it becomes more difficult, individually and collectively, to base identity on a sense of what we are living *for*. The great temptation then is to construct an identity on the basis of who or what we are *against*.

The Need for Enemies

Since World War II, we in the West were taught to believe that we had a great enemy—communism. It was a real and great enemy, and it pulled us together as America led the great anti-communist crusade. Being American meant being against communism. It was an enemy so great that it served to justify defending undemocratic regimes, building an arsenal of nuclear destruction and a vast military-industrial complex while millions of people suffered from poverty, inadequate health care, and schooling.

Through a process as gradual as it was tragic, we became defined by what we were fighting against—more than by what we were for. And when the great enemy fell, the search for new enemies began— the Ayatollah of Iran, Noriega of Panama, Sadaam Hussein of Iraq.

A war against whoever or whatever has provided a basis for summoning sacrifice in a culture where, on a day-to-day basis, most pursue their own self-interest rather than the common good.

However, these enemies were not really great enemies and did not have the power to bind people together in a sense of common purpose, except for a few brief moments when yellow ribbons were tied around trees. It was probably only a question of time before we began to search for the enemies within—the poor, the refugees, single welfare mothers, criminals. Thus the hue and cry: We must defend ourselves against them, they must be controlled. The final twist in this negative dynamic was to make government itself the enemy.

Across the continent we see the growth of gated communities, enclaves and clubs, which are defined not so much by whom they are keeping in but by whom they are keeping out.

The loss of a real, great enemy has also stimulated the creation of virtual enemies. The popularity of shows like *The X-Files* and movies like *Independence Day* is due to the need for enemies. The aliens from another planet seem always somehow in league with people inside the country, the enemies within. The conflict between virtual good and virtual evil has become the sustaining basis of a widespread popular mythology which has made it more difficult for us to identify real evil and real enemies in the world.

The fear of enemies has grown even as America seems to dominate the world more and more. As national borders become increasingly permeable to economic transactions and global communications, the fear of an enemy invading our borders in unseen ways grows daily. It is a fear now substantiated by the attack of September 11. Terrorism has become the new code word for all enemies everywhere. The words spoken by Marlon Brando at the end of the film *The Ugly American* (1963) seem relevant today:

> I'm saying we can't hope to win the Cold War unless we remember what we're for, as well as what we're against. I've learned that I can't preach the American heritage and expect to be believed if I act out of impatience or sacrifice my principles to expediency. I've learned that the only time we're hated is when we stop trying to be what we started out to be, two hundred years ago.

Internal social chaos and disorder can threaten to wreck groups that have little sense of positive purpose and identity. In such cases, the only way a group can be united is through a common agreement that someone else (some other group) is responsible for the social conflicts and problems.

One hears conservatives castigate all the liberals and eco-feminists who are destroying everything society stands for. So too more left-leaning coalitions are composed of the strangest bedfellows who share nothing more than common fear of what they call the vast right-wing conspiracy.

In North America today, governments at every level are tempted to resort to cynical and highly inflammatory tactics as one group after another is excluded from the realm of social responsibility and concern. One wonders how many more scapegoats will be needed, or how long this scapegoating process will go on or how violent it will become. This is easy politics, but, in the long run, it is utterly destructive for any society. It creates a cycle of violence, recrimination and blame, which becomes a social vortex creating ever-new victims. One could say that it destroys any sense of the common good, but it would probably be more true to say that it is indicative of how fragile our sense of social cohesion and common purpose has become.

It must also be said that, at different times and in different places, the churches have defined themselves primarily by what they have been against—with disastrous consequences. Persons and whole groups were scapegoated by the church at those times when it had lost a vision of what it was for and Who it was following. The church defined itself by being against the world and became itself quite worldly. As Hegel once wrote, "When politics is dismissed from the front door of the church it returns again through the sanctuary."

This negative self-definition in the church sometimes took the shape of moral superiority to the enemy, but it may also be present in the attitude of a persecuted minority. It has often been said that the church thrives in situations of persecution in which it is against a dominant political or religious culture. But what happens when the persecution ceases? Witness the fate of the churches in Poland, Quebec, and Ireland. They sustained a great sense of cohesion as long as they could be seen as a place of defense against a threatening culture. Yet there is clearly not enough positive energy in this stance to provide for a sure sense of spiritual energy. The temptation is to continue to act as a persecuted minority, commanding the obedience of members, even if and when the so-called persecutor could care less.

The church cannot simply be against all the evils in a culture. It must also be able to present a vision of what it is for, what life is for, what the point and purpose of the human project are.

One of the oldest Christian heresies was that of Manichean dualism, which divided the world into two separate realms—the world of good and the world of evil. It was a heresy that St. Augustine opposed, and his refutation has become the more orthodox Christian view of the world. He thought that there was no political entity so good that it did not have some shadow world within and that there was no political entity so evil that it did not have some possible points of redemption. His wisdom seems relevant today as we lose sight of the possibility of shadow within ourselves because the sight of a real and great enemy has blinded us.

Living with Purpose

You are not
the recipe for living
the blueprint
for our future
the master plan
for the world.

You are
the Hope in spite
of ourselves
the Love ever
unforeseen
the well of Faith
in the center of the world
in the middle of the day.
You are the Way
the life-long Lifeline
long beyond life.
You are the Life
in our living,
pushing us, pulling us,
pointing us all
in Your direction.
For this we give You thanks.
Amen.

———————————

The absence of a positive sense of meaning is our spiritual crisis, our cultural crisis.

It is possible to see whole cultures as shaped by a defining question or concern. Such a question or concern animates and is reflected in the various structures, symbols, and activities of a culture. So, for example, the ancient and medieval world was preoccupied with the question: What is it that endures? As city-states rose and fell, as whole peoples were devastated by war, they searched for something that would endure in the midst of change.

With the advent of secularization, the predominant question for religious people became "How do we speak about God in an unbelieving world?" This was the question that animated the efforts of the great modern theologians. Yet, this is not the concern in a context such as Latin America because, by and large, faith is not in question there. In that context, the concern is "How do we speak of a God of love to the poor?" How do we say God's love matters, makes a difference now and not only in some heavenly future?

All of these questions are with us still. We see something more than the transient and we seek to understand faith in an unbelieving world and we do not want a God who legitimizes poverty. And the answers that have developed in response to those questions enrich our lives still. We too seek to find something more stable and enduring in the midst of a culture in which everything and everyone seems potentially disposable. We too seek to find a sense of grace in a world in which everything is taken for granted. Nevertheless, we also have a serious and quite specific concern about the question of meaning because of the extent to which we have been carried along by a cultural sense of optimism.

Can we live with a sense of spirited purpose in a culture whose only purpose is simply more? Can we live with a sense of purpose in a culture whose goals have been reduced to the most materialistic and self-centered terms? Or, in more biblical words, can we live *for* the reign of God in a declining empire? Can we live with a sense of what we are for in a culture that has defined itself by what it is against?

It may indeed be true, as the film *The Decline of the American Empire* suggests, that only the saints and mystics live well in a time like this, when there are so few compelling metaphors or models or myths to live by. It is also quite possible that the churches themselves, which are also in a crisis of meaning, are sustained still by the saints and mystics who live within and on the edges of their structures. The more important history of our world and of our churches is written in the lives of the God-given ones.

Nevertheless, I have also been suggesting throughout this book that there is a more ordinary mysticism to be found in discovering the liberating attitude of gratitude. This is not given rarely or only to a few but exists as a present possibility for all of us.

Let me return to some of the considerations that I have attempted to unfold thus far: If and when we stop taking our lives for granted, we can be shocked by the simple awareness that our simple beginning on this earth is nothing short of a miracle. We have not been manufactured, not made, but rather created. We are from God and in this lies our identity and our happiness. I have emphasized the mysterious power of beginnings, because it seems ever more pertinent to a time when some former visions are ending.

To dwell in this mystery is to grow in the sureness that we are created for a reason, a purpose. Our lives were not created to be thrown away or easily disposed of. Just as our lives are much more than things to be consumed or worked on, so too the purpose of our lives cannot be contained by any goal or series of goals.

Consider the story of a man who walked by three men who were laying bricks. "What are you doing?" he asked. The first man said, "I am laying bricks." The second responded, "I am working to make a living for my family." The third man paused and replied, "I am part of building a great cathedral."

I have a sure memory of a catechism book that was given to me when I was smaller and younger. It was a little green book containing a series of questions and answers that were to guide us with certainty in life. Like many, I have forgotten most of those questions and answers and much of the certainty that they promised. However, I do remember the first two questions:

Who made you?

God made me.

Why did God make you?

God made me to show forth his goodness and to be happy
with him forever.

These questions are awesome to me, even now, and the answers seem more than enough to live by. I would probably use
slightly different language today, but is there anything better or
more important to say?

In gratitude we discover our identity and the purpose of our
lives. Such a discovery does not go by the way of definitions and
blueprints. Our identity in God is not something we can easily lay
hold of. It is a mystery we live from and within as surely as we
exist. So too, we can become convinced that we have a purpose in
life, even if we are not always exactly sure what that is. The One
Who Creates is the One Who Redeems is the One Who Sancti-
fies, who concentrates our lives and makes them whole.

A vision of our lives, our sense of the point of our being,
moves through and beyond all the various goals that we set for
ourselves or our culture sets for us. I cannot prove mathematically
that this is so; I believe that this is so.

To recognize our beginnings, our origin in God, helps us
dwell in time and not be consumed by it. In gratitude, the past is
not tossed off but remains a source of power in the present. Indeed, it is gratitude that enables us to truly live in the present moment, to savor the details of daily life, to pay attention rather than
tripping over our lives and ourselves on the way to something else.
The present is more than a fleeting moment, an episode of meaning; it is filled with meaning if we would but attend to it. Patience
is the attentiveness of gratitude. It is also the beginning of contemplation and prayer.

In gratitude we can begin to understand that the purpose of
our lives is not something to be grasped intellectually or con-

trived and constructed. We can trust that there is a meaning to our lives.

It was this trust that enabled John Henry Newman to say the following prayer (which I have paraphrased slightly) during some of the most uncertain and difficult days of his life.

> *You have created me to do some definite service:*
> *You have committed some work to me,*
> *which You have not committed to another.*
> *I have my mission—*
> *I may never know it in this life, but I shall be told it in the next.*
> *I am a link in a chain, a bond of connection between persons.*
> *You have not created me for naught.*
> *I shall do good, I shall do Your work.*

I do not think the meaning of our lives is something we discover through introspection, by looking within ourselves as if there were some *thing* that could be found just by peeling enough layers from the onion of ourselves. In my experience, it appears more in retrospect. As we reconsider our lives, some of the apparently disconnected episodes seem more linked to one another.

Many years ago, I had an experience in a most unexpected place that made it easier for me to believe that individuals' lives have meaning and that this meaning is revealed only in retrospect.

In 1981, a young Jewish woman in Moscow asked me, "Have you ever been to Jerusalem?" She was asking for a reason to hope.

It was a time when a curtain of fear had been pulled around the Soviet Union. The Korean jetliner had just been shot down. Thousands of missiles were ready and aimed around the world. There was a blackout of news and a shutdown of travel to the West.

For those of us on a peace mission to Moscow, this meant only that our return home would be delayed. But for members of the independent peace movement in Russia, the international crisis threatened to become a personal catastrophe.

On the evening of Yom Kippur, I met with members of this group in a dingy Moscow apartment. Most of them had been university professors. That was before they had issued statements saying that the arms race was destroying both superpowers—spiritually and economically. Voices crying in the wilderness. Because of their courageous actions, they had been fired from their university positions and were being forced to clean the streets of their wasteland.

That evening, they talked about the inevitable "knock on the door." Word had spread that the KGB was moving through the fog of fear to round up dissidents. I listened as these intellectual activists talked about the future they could foresee: they would be taken to a "mental hospital" for "treatment." We all knew the euphemisms for what happens with perverse forms of medication, when the mind is turned to mush. These academics knew that there were fates worse than death.

As our meeting drew to a close, Olga went with me to the door and turned to face me. "Have you ever been to Jerusalem?"

"Yes," I answered.

"Tell me what it is like."

A thousand images flashed through my mind, but only one seemed important. "When you drive up to Jerusalem in the spring, you can smell the orange blossoms everywhere." It was a small hope but very real.

She breathed in deeply. It was the scent of hope.

This story has a happy ending. Our peace group was able to get news of the group's "hospitalization" out to various human rights groups in the West. Olga is now teaching in the United States at a small midwestern college.

Had I ever been to Jerusalem? Yes, I had, in the course of doing some research on the Holocaust. The time in Jerusalem had been a significant, even a pleasant, time for me. I thought I had learned something, thought I knew what that experience meant. But I had no idea what it really meant and how much it would mean for others.

It was meant to give hope—in another time and another place—to someone who was afraid that she would lose both her memory and her dreams.

Years later, in addressing a convocation of university students, I was able to assure them that their education had meaning. "I want to assure you that your process of education is significant not only for you but also for others. Sometime, somewhere, someone will turn to you and ask you for a reason to hope. And then everything you have learned, everything you have become will be questioned and summoned forth. I know this will happen at least once in your life."

In the present moment, we may not see or understand the meaning of our lives. However, this does not mean that our lives are meaningless.

To say that God is the point of our being is also to say that the point of our lives extends far beyond death. As once we were created out of nothingness, so once again we will be recreated out of the nothingness of death. This does not mean that what we were and what we have done will be disposed of as so much waste. It means that everything that matters will continue to live in a new way.

The traditional belief in the last judgment was not about the hellfire and brimstone that awaited the big sinners and the little heat reserved for small-time sinners. It was also about the great love that would reveal to us the real consequence of our actions and the true quality of our lives. In the teachings of wise Christians throughout the ages, it was often thought that we would be surprised by the judgment of love. We would come to understand that most of what we thought was sinful was not sinful at all and we would recognize some of the greatest good that we had done, good that had remained hidden from us.

The modern loss of faith in the last judgment ultimately results in a loss of belief in the consequences of one's actions and words, in the consequences of one's life. The unbearable lightness of being, as the novelist Milan Kundera said.

The tragedy is that if we do not think that our actions may have consequences for the worse, then neither will we be convinced that they will make any difference for the better.

Jesus and the Point of His Being

Those of us who are Christians can also remember the example of Someone who lived with a sense of meaning and purpose in the most chaotic and oppressive time. We have only to recall that Jesus lived with God as the point of his being. Again and again, he told his disciples that he had come from God and was going to God. He knew who he was, that his deepest identity lay in the mystery that he was born of God. And he knew that he was *for* God, that he had come to announce the great dream of God, the dream of the reign of God and the great economy of grace.

This was the meaning and purpose of his life. It was his passion. His affirmation of the point of his life was profoundly based on his gratitude for being born of God. This deep connection between gratitude and trust in the future has been simply expressed by Dag Hammarskjold: "For all that has been, Thanks; for all that shall be, Yes."

Jesus has left us with this vision, a vision worthy enough to summon every aspect of our being and the whole of our lives. Yet, this vision is not a blueprint. It is not a detailed plan of what we are to do and how we are to do it. It has been left to us to fill in the blanks, as it were.

The great dream of God for the world is not a concrete plan, but it is compelling. It gives us a sense of how the story of the world and of how our own story will end. It will end as it began— in goodness. It makes all the difference in the world to believe that the dream of God for the world is going to happen.

I learned this from a very holy older woman as she lay dying. Her name was Kieran Flynn. She was a Sister of Mercy who was widely respected for her wisdom about the spiritual life, about life.

Kieran had been diagnosed with multiple melanomas—a particularly virulent and painful form of cancer. She had been taken to Massachusetts General Hospital toward the end of her illness and had been given multiple doses of morphine to ease the pain. Rather quickly she went into complete unconsciousness. What impressed those of us who had gathered around her was that she was almost constantly saying short prayers in a rhythmic, mantra-like fashion: You are the way, You are the truth, You are the life, bless the poor, have mercy. The prayers could not have come from a level of consciousness but had to have come from some deeper level of the unconscious and the imagination. At the deepest level of her being, she had been shaped by the word of God. She was breathing from God and for God and with God. She had become a prayer.

Then one afternoon, as three of us were sitting by her bed in the hospital room, it was as if she awoke but she could not have been conscious. In a very clear voice she said: "I had a dream. I dreamt that all the men and women were all seated around a round table, all equal, all free. It will take a thousand years but it doesn't really matter, because it's going to happen."

And then she slipped back into wherever she had come from. I heard this as the dream of God or what has traditionally been called the vision of the reign of God or the kingdom of God. It is a dream of justice, peace, and love.

Kieran's dream was part of God's great dream for the world. We, each and every one of us, are part of this great dream. Our smaller dreams and hopes are part of God's point for the world. It is sometimes difficult to hear that "it will take a thousand years," but it makes all the difference in the world whether we believe in the power of this dream to prevail. It is this dream that has the power to sustain us in struggle and the power to endure through the collapse of our particular hopes.

───────────────

*You are
the Still Purpose.*

*You come down
as snowflakes onto*

the tops of the mountains.
You flow through the world
as streams and then
as mighty rivers rolling
toward the great ocean
of Your Love.
You sow seeds
of Your purpose
throughout the world
in all nations and peoples
and gather them up again
in Your due season.

You Still Purpose
We begin in Your name
and end in Your name
Amen.

CHAPTER SIX

Living with Spirit

Now I will take stock
for I must go
through the eye of the needle
and along the canal to birth.

I cannot take
the bulk of what I own
what weighs me down
wears me out.

There is room only
for the Love
that has grown
as natural as breathing.

Draw me through the needle
and along the canal to birth.

In the preceding chapters, I have suggested that the spiritual attitude of gratitude releases us from the perpetual dissatisfaction generated by the combined force of an economics of consumerism and the politics of progress. It was also my suggestion that participation in the creative power of God offers the possibility of an alternative to a culture paralyzed, morally and socially, by an ethic of control. It is possible, as the reflections in the previous chapter indicate, to live with a point or purpose to our lives even in a culture that is rapidly losing a positive sense of common purpose and meaning.

The basis of such insights is a faith in God as Creator, as Liberating Power, and as the Spirit among us. They are also based on the conviction that we human beings are most truly ourselves when we act as though we are from God, with God, and for God.

However, I want to acknowledge that such insights are not all that difficult to come by and may come as easily as reading this book. Moments of spiritual revelation are actually rather frequent and happen to many people in the course of their lives, at least once.

What is less usual, and far more significant, is whether we choose to change our lives so that they can be rooted in and founded on such insights. Spirituality does not become whole, substantial, and sustaining until it makes a difference in our lives and in the world.

The wisdom of most of the world's great religions tells us that everything depends on whether we develop habits of being, or virtues, which will help us to live by that which inspires us, helps us breathe more deeply.

Long ago, Aristotle wrote that one learned what justice was by practicing justice, one learned what beauty was by exposing oneself to beauty, and one learned what goodness was by doing good. So too we could say that we learn what gratitude is by acting gratefully. Gratitude can liberate us in this culture, but we must also consciously choose the practices that will liberate gratitude.

This does not mean that we can "work" ourselves into a state of gratitude. However, we can (as the Jewish thinker Martin Buber suggests) "hold ourselves in readiness" for the grace of gratitude. We can develop habits of being that will attune us to the movements of gratitude when they strike a chord within us. Although gratitude as a fundamental attitude is much more than thankfulness for this or that thing, the paradox is that we become an act of gratitude precisely through the practice of daily acts of gratitude.

In the pages that follow, I want to outline some habits of being that can help us live with spirit, with a sense of identity, power, and purpose in a dispirited time and place. These suggestions are not exhaustive, but it is my hope that they will give you some courage to think about which practices would help you liberate gratitude in your life. I can suggest *why* this is important, but you must consider your own context and the particularities of your own life in reflecting on what you *want* to do and why, what you *can* do, and *how* to do it. I have outlined some of the elements that are involved in living with spirit. However, the sequence in which these elements unfold in the process of liberation may vary from person to person, from context to context.

1. Begin before You Are Ready

The previous chapters have already detailed some of the ways in which we can be culturally constrained in our efforts to live a more free and grateful life. We hesitate to choose another way of living because we do not have enough: enough time, enough money, enough energy, enough support, or enough internal strength.

Conviction falters. As the moment of hesitation lengthens, we may halt. It is in this split moment, between wanting the liberation of gratitude and feeling unable or even unwilling to be liberated, that some of the reflections in this book may help steady our wavering spirit. Our sense of being consumed by dissatisfaction is already a grace. Our desire for a different way of life already carries intimations of how to proceed. One of the mysteries of the great economy of grace is that we seek because we have already been found, we ask because we already have the answers placed deep within our soul.

We have enough to go on. We have enough, are enough, to take the next step. It is only our cultural illusions that dictate that we should wait for the perfect moment, the ideal situation, or just the right thing. It is even a religious temptation to think that we must wait, like Saul of Tarsus, to be knocked off our horse with a blinding light before we can take another path.

Some may worry that their efforts will not be "good enough." If so, remember that forgiveness was made for this inevitability. Mistakes will be made, but they are of little account. Forgive yourself and others and begin again.

The old maxim holds true here: The journey of a thousand miles begins with a single step. Faith is like a lantern on a dark path; it shines only far enough to illumine the next step. Only when the next step is taken does the light move on. Our beginning steps in gratitude do not have to be great and grand. They need only be real.

2. Practice Gratitude

What do first steps sound like? What do they resemble?

The beginning of each day is a marvelous opportunity to become more conscious of the awesome mystery of our beginnings in God, to recognize that we can never take our own lives, the lives of others, or the life of the planet and the galaxies we know for granted.

> *Let me awaken into You*
> *Let me lift my arms in praise.*
> *I thank You for this*
> *this once more, this day,*
> *this resurrection.*
> *Let me throw off*
> *the covers of sleep.*
> *I trust You will*
> *wrap me round with goodness.*
> *Let me place my feet*
> *down on You who are*
> *Ground. Grace. Stability of Earth.*
> *Bear me. Bear with me*
> *Bear me forth into*
> *this once more day*
> *this time of my life*
> *You have given me.*
> *Bless me, O Creator*
> *of my beginning.*

Let the water of Your love
run over me, within me.
Shower me with blessing
as I begin this day
in Your name.
Water within water.
Stream of Hope. Ocean of Faith.
Cup me in Your hands
Accept the water of my life
as it flows through this day
Baptize me once again
this day.

———————————

Do not consume these prayers or work at them too hard. Do not feel guilty if you do not say them as often as you had intended. Your desire to be more grateful is already good enough. Give yourself to these prayers or to others like them and let yourself be carried by them.

As we begin each day in gratitude, so too we are invited to end each day in trust. "For all that has been, Thanks; for all that shall be, Yes." It is in the evening that we have the opportunity of reviewing each day in gratitude, of looking back on the day and seeing that it was very good. Difficulties, heartaches, and sufferings will spring to mind and will make it more difficult to be grateful. It may be that there are some realities for which there is no obvious or acceptable reason to be grateful. In these cases, it may be that we can be grateful only for the opportunity to help make the world a place in which it is a little easier to be grateful.

It is in the evening, before we go to sleep, that we are offered the opportunity of letting go, of practicing what it means to entrust our lives to the darkness and the unknown. In a culture dominated by the ethic of control, letting go into the mystery of each night, perhaps entering into the mystery of love, helps us learn how to live more trustingly during the day and to trust that our lives, in the end, will be carried through the ultimate night.

Let them all go to You
    all the joys and sufferings
    of this day.
Let them all go to You
    all the worries of today.
Let them all go to You
    all the mistakes that I made.
Let them all go to You
    all the people that I care for.
Let them all go to You
    all the sufferings of the world.
Let them all go to You.

All the happiness I held
    let it all go to You.
All the good that was done
    let it all go to You.
All the beauty that appeared
    let it all go to You.
All the love that I was given
    let it all go to You.

Let me all go to You.

———————————

Let me go with You
into Your Good Night.
Loosen my grip
on the length of this day.

Lift off the clothes
of these my cares
Unbutton my worries
one by one
Untie the knots
of not being good enough.
Undo the one who is undone.
Cover me with Your Love
Enfold me once again.
Into Your hands
I commend my spirit.
Watch over my dear ones
the near ones and the far ones
Eyes of my eyes.
Hear the strangers who cry
Ears of my ears.
Hold them all close
while I am asleep
Heart of my heart
Mind of my mind
Mind them. Mind me.
Mend us all in the great womb
of Your dear darkness
once again.

———————————

During the day there are countless opportunities to catch our breath, as it were. At these times we can become more conscious of being from God and for God as we breathe more slowly in and out. This simple exercise helps us to re-situate our lives, to place them in touch with the source of our power and the point of our being.

There are some breathing exercises that emphasize the breathing *in* of good energy and the breathing *out* of unhealthy energy or that ask us to imagine breathing *in* positive energy and breathing *out* positive energy into the world. This can be most helpful. However, it also can tend to divide our breathing between the inner and outer worlds.

I am suggesting that, for those of us who have grown up with a more linear sense of our lives, it may also be helpful to situate each breath of our lives within the longer breathing of our lives *from* God and *for* God. This is the source of our breath, our spirit, our inspiring.

> *Still*
> *I breathe in You*
> *You breathe in me*
> *I live in You*
> *You live in me*
> *I come from You*
> *I go to You*
> *You in the beginning*
> *You in the end*
> *From You*
> *With You*
> *For You*
> *Forever.*
> *Amen.*

These simple words, repeated until we become a prayer, serve to re-situate our lives, to liberate our desire for gratitude and our conviction of its possibility even in the midst of great cultural captivity.

Meals can become the occasion for gratitude rather than the time for eat-and-run consumerism.

> *We give You thanks*
> *for You sustain us*
> *with real food*
> *and real drink.*
> *You nourish us*

with friends as real as food
with joy as clear as water
with love as good as this meal.
This is enough.
We do not ask for more.
This is more than enough
reason to bless Your name
Forever.
Make us always mindful of those
who do not have enough
food and friendship
water and love and joy.
Give them enough
that they too may be thankful
Amen.

Then too there are the simple words of thanks that we can bestow as blessings on those near and far, words that can become effortless and graceful with practice. Thank you for helping, thank you for doing what you could, thank you for being here once again.

I recall the enthusiasm with which one of our refugee children from Latin America greeted a volunteer who came in once a week to help as a receptionist. In the morning, the little girl would squeal with delight, "Today Sue, today Sue!" That morning Sue would delight in the fact that she was not being taken for granted. "Wouldn't it be lovely," Sue reflected, "if my own kids woke up saying, 'Today Sue!' . . . and wouldn't it be great if I woke up every day saying, 'Today kids!'"

Such thoughts of gratitude for those near and dear frequently flit through our mind—but it is only in expressing those thoughts, in word or action, that they deepen as a groove in our mind.

Nevertheless, it takes an even more conscious effort to express our gratitude for people whom we do not know personally, who live at some remove from our daily lives. At one point in my life, I

realized that I was occasionally grateful for something a public fig-
ure had done, was impressed and encouraged by the actions of
those whom I had heard of only second or third hand, moved by
the courage of someone half a world away. I began the habit of
writing thank-you notes to strangers, usually at the beginning of a
new year. I did not churn out hundreds of form letters but simply
wrote a few as sincerely as I could. Almost invariably my letters
were answered by yet another thank-you note. In the great economy of grace, gratitude grows as it is expressed and shared.

In my work with refugees, I have discovered that many of
them so want to say thank you in some way. However, given the
severe financial and other limitations that constrain them, they
often fret over their inability to adequately express their gratitude.
They seem to feel liberated from their own burden of ingratitude
when I tell them that they will be able to be express that gratitude
fully, at some point in their lives, perhaps on a day when a stranger
in need comes to their door. Such a perspective is important for
each one of us at moments when we feel unable to express our
gratitude fully. The moment will arise when what we have received will grow not so much in giving in return but in giving to
another person in another situation.

It is also helpful to take some longer time for gratitude. Traditionally the Sabbath was such a time, but it too has been sacrificed
to the demands of consumerism. This does not mean that the
spirit of the Sabbath cannot be reclaimed. We need time to enjoy
all those realities in our lives that we can be grateful for, that we
can look upon and see that they are very good. We need time for
family and friends, even time to relish the successes in our works
and projects. There must be time in our lives when we can allow
ourselves to be nourished and sustained by the goodness that we
so quickly pass by on the way to somewhere else.

All of these simple acts of gratitude lie within the reach of possibility for each one of us—whether rich or poor, sick or in good
health. However, even such simple practices of gratitude once
started are difficult to sustain beyond an initial desire and convic-

tion. The moment of gratitude can be overwhelmed by the thousand other moments in the day when the concerns of having more than less, the feelings of being less than more, dominate and diminish our spirits.

3. Gather with Like-Spirited People

The illusion that liberation means autonomy, freedom from all the exterior influences of who or what is other than ourselves, is one of the greatest ties that binds us in this culture. Isolated, alone with ourselves or a few friends and family members, we will be overpowered by the sheer all-pervasive force and influence of the culture of dissatisfaction. Our only escape will be some kind of refuge among those we love, some kind of haven in our hobbies, some sanctuary in the wilderness or in the interior labyrinth of ourselves.

While it is important that we learn to distinguish who we are from others, it has become ever more important in this culture to identify the deep relationships that connect us with others and with all living things. We cannot be liberated alone. Gratefulness grows in relationship, in community, and in communion.

In chapter four, I suggested that power, even the conviction that we have power, arises when we are in a dynamic relationship with other people. Being with others is a condition for liberating gratitude.

What are the names of these others?

One could begin by reviewing the various groups, associations, or networks in which one already participates. Are they organized as ways of doing more or being more, as ways of escape or forms of relief? Are they driven by the culture of dissatisfaction? Do they make me feel even more powerless and guilty than I already am? Are they organized more in terms of what they are against than in terms of what they are for? If the answer to any or all of these questions is in the affirmative, then such groups will probably not be much help in the liberation of gratitude.

However, more questions need to be asked. Are there times when I feel that this group wants to address some of the roots of my/our dissatisfaction in a deeper way? Are there moments when I can relax with who I am and what I have? Are there ways in which this group helps me feel that together we can initiate something or change some of our present realities? Does this group see itself connected with other groups or responsive to something or someone greater than itself? If the answer to any or all of these questions is even somewhat affirmative, then there is just the possibility that within one's present fabric of relationships there is the potential for liberation.

Prepare to be surprised by the results of such an assessment. It may lead you to question the value of some of your favorite groups or some associations you have worked long and hard to belong to. On the other hand, it may lead to a new appreciation of some of your more taken-for-granted relationships.

A sports team one has been involved in for years may suddenly seem either dispiriting or a potential source of new energy. A job may become even more of a job or may reemerge in our imaginations as worthy of our finest efforts. A book club may strike us as just another form of escape or may become a new opportunity to discuss what really matters. A group committed to justice may be unmasked as nothing more than an exercise in legitimizing all dissatisfaction or it may take on new passion formed by a vision of an alternative social model. A spirituality group may be revealed as a lifestyle enclave or may resurface as the locus of a much wider and deeper relationship with the world. A church group (such as a service group or bible study group) may take on new significance either as a defensive little bastion of righteousness or as the ground of our winging toward goodness.

Such an assessment can invite us to reconsider what priority we give to which groups, how much time and energy we invest in them. Usually there are some already existing groups or relationships in our lives that have the potential to liberate gratitude. What is needed is the time and attention to make this potential more of a reality.

However, it is also possible that a review of our various involvements and relationships may produce results that are not all

154 ──────────────────── Living with Spirit

that promising. In this case, we must make some effort to seek out like-spirited people. In the beginning there must be a gathering of energy.

This may mean putting out a question or invitation on the Internet. What happens when spirituality is big business? Has anyone met a truly grateful person? It may mean placing a provocative question by the office cooler: Do you have a house for your car? How much is just a little bit more? If we are being just, then why are we all so unhappy? It may mean hosting an evening for some people who might be interested in discussing this book.

Find some way of identifying those who share your questions, concerns, and desires and gather together with them. At some point, in whatever words are most appropriate, together you may ask: What can we do to help each other liberate gratitude? This may lead to other forms of interaction: a phone call a day, a chat room that provides a space for interaction, a gathering in the morning for a few minutes of meditation before the day begins, taking on some form of service together, developing lists of books and other resources that encourage us to think about ways of doing things that don't simply follow the cultural drift toward having more and being more.

If such initiatives are stillborn or fizzle out, you could search out existing groups that you think could help you live more gratefully, could increase your sense of creative power, or could help you take the point and purpose of your being more seriously. Such groups may lie close at hand or they may require a longer journey—either literally or figuratively. This may involve taking a course, which may help you think off the path you have usually taken when thinking about economics, politics, or even religion. It may mean helping to build a house for Habitat for Humanity, thus experiencing yourself as capable of participating in the construction of something new and worthwhile. It may mean joining a group that does something that does not compute. It may mean volunteering with an organization in which people seem to give without counting the cost.

Whatever the case, however you find your place with like-spirited people, you will have a greater possibility of becoming more liberated in every way.

In effect, we need to find what the Czech playwright and president Vaclav Havel called a "parallel culture." His insights were formed by the experience of trying to live an alternative to the dominance of materialism as it was associated with the Soviet form of communism. He had come to the conclusion that it was an illusion to think that one could ever live totally outside such a dominant culture in some romantic counterculture. He realized that the line between the dominant culture and the alternative to it is not simply outside oneself, out there as a clear option between two political systems. The line goes through each one of us, he wrote, to the extent that we participate in a dominant culture and have a faint desire for some different way of living. He doubted that it was possible to see through the lies of the dominant culture, through its false promise of happiness (you will be happy if you have a job and enough things), as long as one is fully immersed in that culture.

He thought, quite rightly in my estimation, that most people do not dream of changing the way things are until something different becomes more attractive and more possible. We do not take the first step on a different path until we think there is something to land on.

In a telling remark, after the fall of communism, Havel said that "materialism may have failed as an ideology in the East but it has certainly triumphed as a matter of fact in the West."

In the context of the former Soviet Union, the "parallel culture" took shape through underground universities in which the views of Plato and others were hotly debated, in plays that took place before audiences gathered in secret, in the poetry, novels, and essays produced by the *samizdat* press, in forms of devotion and the bible study taking place in the catacombs of communism, in the political debates of labor unions and various professional groups. It was in this culture that it was possible to begin to "live in the truth" in a culture of lies and misinformation.

This parallel culture grew in strength until it reached a point where the people felt clear enough to take to the streets with candles. And then, quite suddenly, the whole system of lies collapsed like a house of cards. Not because of the great military victory of the West, not because the Soviet Union had lost the nuclear arms race, but simply because a significant number of its own people said clearly that they didn't believe in the lies any more, they didn't believe that simply having more things and a job would make them happy. They wanted something to believe in, something to hope in, something worth living for and worth dying for, some great point and purpose in their lives.

A decade later we know that much of this great hope came to naught and the alternative vision was quickly swallowed up by ever more crass forms of materialism. For so many in the former Soviet Union, freedom means nothing more than shopping. The more some go shopping, the less many are able to purchase even the basic necessities of life.

It would be easy to dismiss Havel's reflections on the importance of a parallel culture as valiant but misguided. Nevertheless, it is also possible to learn that it may well take a much longer time to develop an alternative to a materialistic way of life than he thought. One of the most serious questions for political and social thinkers today must be: What are the conditions today for the development of an alternative to the dominant culture? My purpose in writing this book is not so much to answer that question as to indicate why it is becoming increasingly urgent and why it deserves our attention.

4. Live More Simply

It would seem obvious that liberation in a culture driven by the craving for more would somehow involve the choice to live with less. Indeed, an increasing number of people seem to be advocating a simpler lifestyle—"Live simply so that others may simply live" as the bumper sticker says. The foundation for this apt maxim seems to be the rather accurate assessment that while some have more than enough, many have less than enough. Such awareness assumes that the lifestyle we choose does affect other people, that if some have more of the pie, others have less. Good people, it is assumed, will give some of what they have so others can have more.

However, in America, the North and the West, looking out for yourself and yours is seen as civic virtue. This is the height of independence and responsibility. Looking out for your family, for example, is seen as morally good, but looking out for those beyond your natural circle of concern is more a matter of debate. It becomes less a question of what one wants to do and more a question of what one should do.

Unfortunately, exhortations to live a simpler lifestyle are often dished out with great dollops of guilt. In the process, the giver is increasingly consumed with a sense that he or she can never give enough or live simply enough to be good enough. The one who receives, more often than not, is also demeaned, marked as someone who is defined by the fact that he or she does not have enough. In spite of many good intentions, the choice to live more simply can become yet another manifestation of the culture of dissatisfaction. As such, it holds little promise of liberation.

However, something much more dynamic and liberating begins to happen when a sense of gratitude and freedom coincides with the awareness that "it is enough." It means setting some kind of limit, not so much to restrain oneself as to curb the insatiable demands of the consumer culture. To say "it is enough" is to enter into a very different state of being in which the desire to live more simply becomes an act of gratitude rather than guilt.

There is a story told of the great medieval mystic Teresa of Avila that illustrates the kind of freedom I am alluding to. It seems she had hanging in her room a picture of Jesus that was set in a gold frame. One night Teresa awoke with a great sense of guilt and was seized with a sense that the frame was too expensive and that perhaps she should give it away as she had taken a vow of poverty. However, she soon heard a "voice" that said: "Do whatever leads to love." The next day she reflected on the voice in the night and knew that a simpler lifestyle made sense only in the context of the economy of love. In other words, if having the gold frame helped her to become more loving, then she would keep it. If the gold frame made her less loving, then she would give it away. A more loving person, of course, would more easily tend to give of her very self and to give many things away in the process.

Similarly, it is helpful to consider what it is that we have and want that will lead us to greater gratitude and what it is that will hinder the liberation of gratitude in our lives. What kinds of sexual relationships leave us feeling ever more dissatisfied and which ones leave us feeling content and grateful? What are the situations in which we can give ourselves freely and when do we feel driven to perform in better, faster, more effective ways? What type of work is deeply satisfying and which form of work leaves us feeling ever more driven? Finally, how much do we really need to be happy?

Such questions are difficult to answer alone, because we are all rather thoroughly conditioned to think that we will always need more than we have to be happy. I remember a rather poignant time when I was acting as a resource person for a group of teachers who were being offered more money for more overtime. When I asked them to list what they wanted most in their lives at the present moment, almost all said they wanted more time with their family and friends. Many expressed great concern about how the stress of their job was affecting their relationships. Nevertheless, very few of them felt able to pass up the opportunity for a little more cold hard cash. The extra money, they reasoned, would make things a little easier and happier for their family. These were good people, but they were not happy.

These teachers needed some group of like-spirited people, some parallel culture that would help to strengthen their conviction that their family would be much happier if they had more time together rather than more money to share. We all need others to help us sort out what true happiness means. It is through interacting with like-spirited people that we grow in a sense that we have the power to change the conditions that are contributing to our unhappiness. Fortunately, increasing numbers of people are questioning their driven way of life and have a partially formed hope that happiness lies in another way.

Here again, the journey of a thousand miles begins with a single step. We have only to make one small decision to say "it is enough" and the next step will get easier.

Our own unhappiness, I have suggested in previous chapters, is intimately linked to the unhappiness of others. It is not so much that we are the cause of the unhappiness of others (such as the poor and the destitute) but that we are all chained by the false promises of a culture of dissatisfaction. We are involved in the liberation of each other.

From my own perspective, as I watch refugees receiving "donations" from many and various people, I know there is a difference when one gives out of gratitude or guilt. When someone brings clothes, freshly washed and ironed, out of joy in giving these away, then the refugee who receives them puts on dignity and grace as the clothes are worn. This becomes even more true when there is a relationship of friendship and respect between a good neighbor and the refugee who has no clothes for the winter. In the process, the refugee becomes more than an object of concern and is reinstated as a person with a face and a name.

Liberating gratitude involves much more than living simply, but it includes at least that.

5. Look for Good Examples

In his reflections on violence, Gil Baillie has argued rather convincingly that we learn a great deal by imitating others. Our fundamental attitudes are not formed in splendid isolation but in the course of watching what others do and say. He cites the example of children in a medieval town who watched the hanging of a so-called witch. The next day they placed their dolls in nooses and hung them from sticks. In watching violence, they began to replicate the patterns of violence within themselves.

If he is right, and I think he is, then one of the most important decisions we have to make is whom we will imitate. That we will imitate someone is not in doubt, but who that is can remain our choice.

The culture of consumerism offers us many models to imitate. Advertising extends daily enticements to imitate those who are going faster, getting better, and becoming more beautiful. Those who fashion advertisements seem to understand very well the power of what the Greeks called *mimesis* or imitation. Millions of people who may think of themselves as quite independent now wear jeans as they imitate a new ideal of casual comfort.

If we are genuinely interested in living an alternative to the driven and somewhat pointless life of a culture of dissatisfaction, then we will need to search for some good examples to imitate. We need to discover some real people or groups that seem to exemplify what living in gratitude means. We do not need many models, extraordinary examples, or large and overwhelming instances of liberating gratitude. But we do need them to be real.

Scroll through your memory and see whom you can identify as a grateful, free, and happy person. I believe that each of us knows or has met at least one such person in our lives. We can learn how to become more grateful by recalling how they acted, what they did and said. There may even be someone close at hand who is part of your life at the moment. This person can become your teacher in the ways of liberating gratitude. I have met, for example, a woman who is completely happy tending a very large garden in northern Ontario. I also know a businessman who made the decision that he had made enough money and now wanted to give at least half of his time to helping small groups engaged in community development economics. These are real people. I learn by watching what they do.

It is also possible that the teacher may be someone you read about, someone you saw in a movie or heard at a conference. I have listened to more than one young person who went to a talk given by Jean Vanier, the founder of the L'Arche communities for the disabled. "I would like to be like him," they have said, or words to that effect.

Such good examples of gratitude can be found anywhere, sometimes in the most surprising places—among the poor, in wards for the terminally ill. One of our young volunteers learned the most important lesson in her life as she was caring for a refugee who was dying from the complications of severe diabetes. Alone, far away from his family and his culture, he spent his days giving thanks for the loveliness of the moment and the graciousness of those who cared for him. In truth, everyone who tended to him became more gracious and lovely because of his attitude of gratitude.

I am also now convinced that examples of gratitude can be found in any culture and in any of the great religious traditions. God has not left us without teachers, without witnesses to grace. We have only to find them—and even our desire to find them is already its own grace.

As a Christian I take Jesus as the great example of gratitude. I believe I can become more grateful in the imitation of Christ. There are no shortcuts in this regard. In order to understand what Jesus meant by gratitude we must live as he lived, do what he did. He continually blessed the God who was in his beginning and who was the point of his being. The power Jesus exercised was the power to create a new beginning, a new way of living and imagining the world that was according to the great economy of grace. He taught us that what we give away, including the gift of ourselves, grows and multiplies in the giving. He invited us to believe in a world transformed by the graciousness of giving. Love one another…especially those who do not have enough. This was his truth. He was happy and unafraid. Blessed.

To those who believed in his creative power he gave the power to walk tall and straight, to see and hear anew. In this power, he forgave and made it possible for someone, something new to begin again. His was the power of liberating gratitude—called Salvation and Resurrection.

We who would seek to learn from him and imitate his ways should not wait until we are ready. Once again he calls to us from the shores of our lives. Do not wait until you are grateful to follow me. Live with me, as I live, and you will learn what it means to be grateful.

We could read the gospel again, as if for the first time, as the good example of gratitude. Many of us have listened to it so often, have heard it misquoted and distorted so often, that we classify it as obsolete. While it is true that the gospel may be no longer novel, it is also possible for it to become genuinely new.

6. Think with the Mind of Your Heart

Throughout this book I have been situating gratitude as an all-encompassing attitude toward life and the world. Gratitude withers when it becomes another form of self-development, a feeling of personal peace that acts as a protective buffer against the currents of culture. If gratitude is only a feeling, no matter how strong and significant it may be, it will become as fleeting as feelings sometimes are when faced with the apparent solidity of what is called "reality." I have met people who have been truly inspired by a weekend workshop on gratitude and then returned to work on Monday to the same old forms of captivity. Some of the reasons for the failure of a feeling of gratitude to take hold and transform a life have been discussed in the previous reflections on powerlessness and isolation.

However, the general inclination to lapse toward ingratitude is also related to the rather limited view of gratitude as a feeling. One of the more unfortunate legacies of the Enlightenment has been the tendency to separate feelings and thinking in a dualistic way. Once this split is assumed, the question becomes whether feeling or thinking is a more superior way of knowing. The question can reappear in terms of gender claims about whether the female or male way of knowing is superior.

This dualism fails to recognize the deep and intimate connection between feeling and thinking. It would be more true to say that all our feelings are thoughtful assessments of reality and that our feelings can be called inappropriate if they do not correspond to reality. It is also true, in my experience, that a change in perceptions and ideals can result in a real change in feelings. For example, if I learn about all the toxins in the river flowing by, I might not be so inclined to feel the loveliness of it all.

If gratitude is to grow into an all-encompassing attitude, it must become whole at that point where feelings and thinking co-incide. In other words, we must begin to think through what it would mean to take gratitude as the basic starting point in our worldview. It would mean thinking through and beyond the kinds of economics and politics that begin by taking life for granted, that begin by believing that more is better, that begin by assuming that if some have more others must inevitably have less.

In short, we need to find the ideas, the theories, the models of society and the images of politics that are deeply coherent with an attitude of gratitude. We cannot simply say "Thank you, Jesus" and then continue to act in a controlling and competitive way in the world of business. It is not enough to feel grateful. We are not fully liberated until we think grateful, imagine grateful, act grate-ful. This is when gratitude becomes a whole, or holy, attitude.

There is more than one way of thinking about economics, more than one way to imagine the dynamics of a society. When, finally, we have become dissatisfied with our dissatisfied culture, we may have this felt thought: *There must be another way.* Very thoughtful economists and sociologists understand this and are much more humble in their remarks about "the economy" and its demands. They understand that if human beings have shaped their economies, it is also human beings who can change them.

Until we think through our feelings of gratitude, they will re-main cut off and isolated from the wider world in which we live and move and have our being. What would it mean to take our astonishment at the wonder of life as the starting point for our social and economic worldview? What would it mean to take our radical gratitude for the earth as the starting point for evaluating globalization?

It is not the purpose of this book to develop the details of so-cial and economic alternatives to the culture of dissatisfaction. However, this task is essential, and one in which each of us must engage. We do not need to be experts in "economics" to begin to think about what is happening to human beings in this materialis-tic culture. Even if we don't understand some of the theories of economics, we do not have to bow down and worship them in their incomprehensibility.

We must question the so-called experts in economics and politics, and we must ask them to justify their assumptions. A very fine professor once told me that if someone really understands something then that person is able to say it simply in a way that everyone can understand. Why then do so few people seem to be able to understand the world of economics that shapes us daily and on every level of our being? Experts and non-experts alike, we need to be liberated from our rigid assumptions about the way things are and are meant to be.

All over the world, there are people trying to find practical alternatives to the driven and consuming way of life. Seek them and they will be found. Listen to them and you will find your hope strengthened.

In the city where I live, there is a small but very real example of a group of people who have tried to think differently about the way our lives are organized economically. Within this group are businessmen who are used to talking the bottom line and a poet called Joy Kogawa who came to her own conclusion that economics did not have to be based on greed. Within a sixteen-square-block area of downtown Toronto the group has created a zone of neighborhood businesses that use an alternate currency, called the Toronto dollar. One-tenth of every dollar used is funneled back into the community development projects of that area. The point of this economic arrangement is not only profit; it is also about people, about building a sustainable community of people. Interestingly enough, the only businesses that will not accept the Toronto dollar are the liquor stores.

Joy Kogawa isn't an expert in economics, but she had a great personal investment in building human community. Because of this she had a passion to understand why so many people were becoming less human as capitalism became more competitive. She kept asking the question, "Is there another way?" until some people gathered together to begin to help her answer the question. Together they thought with the minds of their hearts.

7. See from the Center and the Edge

Thinking about economics and politics is a critical affair, but it is also part of the process of constructing positive alternatives to the culture of dissatisfaction. Such critical thinking can be learned from teachers and books but is best taught, I think, by those who stand to benefit the least from the present economic arrangement. In the course of this book I have suggested that hardly anyone really benefits as a human being from the present economic culture in which we live and that all are somewhat diminished in the process. However, it is most obvious in the lives of the very poor and destitute whose casualties are the most taken for granted. We cannot think holistically until we understand what it feels like to be dismissed as an acceptable loss in the great cultural scheme of things. Ultimately, we are all "acceptable losses" in the culture of consumerism, but the poor know this ahead of time, as it were. Theirs is a crucified wisdom. Where you live determines what you see. The people you listen to influence what you hear.

Do you have a house for a car?

8. Be Connected to a Longer Tradition, a Wider Community

Because ingratitude has such a grip on us, it is not easy for us to loosen into gratitude, to discover a way of liberating gratitude. We are constrained, as I mentioned in chapter five, by all the ideologies of empire that lead us to imagine ourselves as the center of the world: ME, HERE, NOW.

If we believe that NOW is really the most advanced and human way to be, then we will all too easily dismiss who and what has gone before us as obsolete. NOW is better than THEN and BEFORE and all that's HISTORY and TRADITION. This is quite tragic, for we lose our knowledge of the past, a knowledge that could help us see that much of what we assume is so novel and new has actual parallels in the past. There have been great empires that rose and fell and we know some of the signs of an empire in decline.

The past has its horrors, at times tormented by demons with a human face and twisted by ignorance beyond belief. NOW is better than that THEN. However, the past also holds the memories of those times when genuine alternatives to the dominant culture did emerge. To read something of the past is to learn that there have been cultures that attempted to have their economic and social dynamics shaped by more spiritual and human concerns. There have been cultures formed by an overarching sense of purpose that generated passion, brilliance, beauty, and inventiveness, cultures that could ask for sacrifice from their citizens. There have been moments in the West when the power of truth and the spirit were more valued than the power of military or economic might. There have been cultures that valued creative power more than the power of control.

If we know this was true THEN, it makes it more possible to imagine this happening NOW. It is only with an imagination flattened by the imperious NOW that it does not seem "realistic" to think of alternatives.

We tend to treat various epochs of the past as mere stepping-stones to the present. The past is doomed to obsolescence, or so we are inclined to believe in the consumer culture—until it reappears as the latest fad or in the kind of nostalgia that binds us more surely to the present sense of dissatisfaction.

Yet, the past flows forward, as it were, as burden and blessing, and we cannot have the one without the other.

The history of the church is also potentially both problematic or promising for Christians. Whatever the case, it is a little more difficult for Christians to erase the past from the screen of their minds because our faith is rooted in historical events. We must bear the burdens of the sins of the church's past, the moments when it became a community of control rather than a community of blessing. However, the history of the church, its tradition, is also potentially liberating for a culture that is stuck in the NOW of life. We have much to learn from the wisdom of Christian communities who lived through times of cultural decline and rebirth. We need to remember the mysterious action of the Spirit who initiates new beginnings at times of endings.

The very notion of tradition presumes that the present is not some sacred point of reference. And so the conventional wisdom of empire looks on some church teachings and sees them as "authoritarian," "out of date," and "out of touch with our reality." That is to say, irrelevant to ME, HERE, NOW. Yet, it is precisely the sense of community, the perspective of the wider world, and the long sense of history that we most desperately need as a countervailing attitude to the ideologies of empire. We need some other point of reference from which we can act, one based on the realities of the WE of ALL PLACES and ALL TIMES.

For all of us who are mired in the NOW, it is important to place ourselves in relationship to the generations that will follow. We are indeed part of a great chain of being that ties us to the future of this earth. Aboriginal peoples have taught us that, in every decision, we must always take into account how that decision will affect seven generations after us.

This was the kind of consideration that led Dietrich Bonhoeffer to make the fateful choices he did during the Nazi era. He did not use his own moral purity as the point of reference for his decisions. Rather, he asked himself how his decision would affect the next generation. Would it leave them with a future to hope in?

We must find ways of allowing ourselves to be drawn beyond present considerations of the here and now. Look into the eyes of a child. Watch a child wrapped in the sleep of trust. Let the little children, and the teenagers and the young adults, lead us. It is their world more than it is ours.

Being connected to past and future generations is what it means to be part of the "communion of saints." We are not alone. We are in a living relationship to those who have gone before us and to those who will follow after. Will future generations rise up and call us blessed?

We must also discover ways of letting our lives be stretched beyond the HERE, the limitations of our cultural experience. There is a world out there that is not like ours. It is not necessarily better or worse but it is different and in that difference is liberation from another aspect of the imperial ideology of ME-HERE-NOW.

Travel, when it is more than another form of consumerism, can be liberating in this regard. We can discover like-hearted people in places beyond the world that we know. These connections can liberate power in a wider context. In the Christian tradition, the relationship of Christian communities throughout the world was called the sign of catholicity, in the widest sense of that term. It is important to know that it is not all up to us. We are part of a wider and deeper community of spiritual power that we can count on. For Christians in North America, who take on the immense moral burden of their times, this is a liberating realization.

We must learn the modesty of the biblical tradition, which acknowledges that we are not the center of the world. Unlike the protagonists of empire, we do not see ourselves as the source of solutions for the rest of the world. And, unlike the critics of empire who nonetheless remain bound by its perspective, we do not see ourselves as the cause of all the problems of the world. Here and now we need to reclaim and rethink the values of tradition, community, and genuine authority while criticizing false traditionalism, destructive institutionalism, and authoritarianism.

9. Find a Beloved Community

We are living in a culture that is now defined by a powerful vision of who and what it is against. We are at war with terrorism. This may be true, but it is not enough to live by. The danger, as I have mentioned in the previous chapter, is that we will become like that which we fight against.

Thus, it becomes ever more imperative to be grounded in a positive sense of who or what we are for. We must find what the Appalachian poet and essayist Wendell Berry calls "a beloved community."

He has written "manifestoes" against some of the policies of his government and the practices of his culture. However, he too has seen the peril of being only against his nation or culture. In order to criticize these realities, he knows he must be rooted in a beloved community. For him, this is the little village, the small space of earth and land called Port Royal in Kentucky. It is not a perfect place, but it is the community in which he is rooted and located, and he has great affection for it. According to Berry, only when thinking is guided by affection does it become real and true. From his perspective in this beloved country he can criticize his nation and not become like that which he is fighting against. From this perspective, he can also truly say (and with an affection that is not blind loyalty) "I love my country." It is here that he is grateful:

> Like a tide it comes in,
> wave after wave of foliage and fruit,
> the nurtured and the wild,
> out of the light to this shore.
> In its extravagance we shape
> the strenuous outline of enough.

So too, I think Christians need to be located in a "beloved community"—where we are at peace and in place. This could be a plot of land, but it can also be a set of streets, a neighborhood, a place of worship, a community of commitment, a bible study group—wherever we know the gospel is really "good news," wherever our faith is the affection that guides our thinking. Located in a beloved community, we may truly say: "I am grateful for the givenness of this culture. I am blessed to be a Christian. I am privileged to be a member of the church."

My beloved community is a little street called Wanda Road, which is located in the larger metropolitan area of Toronto. It is here that I live with refugees and it is here that good neighbors have welcomed us. We now have an annual street party and on that one night it is as if the veil is drawn apart for a few hours and we know who and what we are called to be. It is not a perfect street, but I have a great affection for it. My truest words and thoughts, my deepest perceptions, flow from this affection. It is here that I find the courage to be critical of my culture—because I know how much I love it.

10. Contemplate the Face of the World

Wendell Berry has gone local because of what he sees as the dangers of the vast and rampaging forces of globalization. A similar concern has moved others to get more globally connected in an alternative sort of way. As the borders of nation-states are weakening, there are simultaneous and sometimes opposing movements toward the local and the global.

We do not yet know whether the movement toward globalization will be ultimately humanizing or dehumanizing. This is the struggle of our century—determining whether we will be connected for the better or the worse.

There are those who think that the benefits of a global economy and new communications technology will eventually trickle down to the benefit of all. Meanwhile, there are others who are connecting on a global scale to resist these forces. Demonstrations at World Trade Organization meetings are now a normal feature of our times.

While corporations and the new anti-globalization forces may differ in their assessments of the realities of globalization, they both share a common tendency to abstract from the particularities of life. In the cost/benefit analysis of the corporations and in the litanies of injustice recited by the anti-globalization forces the unique outline of a particular face, the cadence of language, and the geography of real hope are lost. Globalization is faceless and nameless. Impersonal. This can be only dangerous.

Some of the most interesting spiritual responses to the process of globalization attempt to connect persons and groups to the energies of the universe. These spiritualities of interconnectedness move beyond the rather individualistic spiritualities that have characterized our culture. However, these spiritualities of interconnectedness, because they rely heavily on an organic model of understanding, tend toward abstraction from the particularities of place, from the bodily burden of suffering. In discussions about processes, networks, and issues, the name is lost, the eyes are lost, the person is lost.

Our challenge is to live spiritually in a way that is really located in this world, in our own time and place, and to be connected to the wider world without becoming vague and abstract in the process.

It is here that the reality of the Cosmic Christ may be helpful, at least for Christians. It is the person of Jesus Christ who has become for Christians the mysterious bond between the local and the global, between the realities of being incarnate in a particular culture and alive everywhere and for all time. In the mystery of Christ, we are united to all people everywhere in a personal way. As the poet Gerard Manley Hopkins put it: "Christ plays in ten thousand places, lovely in limbs, and lovely in eyes not his."

In the twenty-first century, we are called to a new form of contemplation, to a way of mysticism that allows us to see the world as more than an object, as something quite other than ourselves yet which is, nonetheless, eminently personal.

In Christ we are united with others in a personal rather than an abstract way. Those who suffer in the mines of Colombia are carrying his cross. Those who are dying of thirst in the Sonora Desert cry out as he did. "Jesus is in agony until the end of the world," as Pascal said. And Jesus is also resurrecting until the end of the world, beginning again and again in small, fresh hopes. This is not an abstract universal process of dying and rising. It is a mystery with a name and a face.

There is a saying that we must think globally and act locally. It may be more accurate to say that we must be able to think locally (with affection) if our global thinking is to be true. We are also called to contemplation, to see the face of the world and to love it beyond all attempts to deface it.

The reflections of Thomas Merton, the monk and mystic, are helpful in this regard. In his contemplative vision of the suffering of the world, he moved beyond generalities and abstractions and restated the reality of global suffering in personal terms.

In the whole world, throughout the whole of history, even
among religious men and among saints, Christ suffers dis-
memberment...All over the face of the earth the avarice
and lust of men breed unceasing divisions among them, and
the wounds that tear us from union with one another widen
and open out into huge wards. Murder, massacres, revolu-
tion, hatred and slaughter and torture of the bodies and
souls of men, the destruction of cities by fire, the starvation
of millions, the annihilation of populations...Christ is
massacred in His members, torn limb from limb...

The thousands of bits of information, the countless sound bites,
are gathered and become a face and a name: Jesus Christ. It is this
Person who summons us to respond to the world, as it is ending
and beginning anew. Our responses will vary, but we must respond: to stand at the foot of the cross, to help carry a cross, or to
work for justice so that no one will ever be put on a cross again.

————————

We pray to You
because You are not
a pure idea
a perfect equation
a nameless energy
a vague love.

You have had history with us,
We have had words.
We know You can be touched.
You hear our cry and bend down
bend over backwards for us.

You have watched with admiration
as we created something with our lives.
You have talked with us as a friend,
You have faced us.
In You we have seen our face.
You. Most Personal One.
And so we pray to You.
To You. Tu. Du. Su.

———————

There are surely many more ways to practice gratitude and such wisdom is important for all of us to share—for the practice of gratitude has become the habit of holiness in this time and in this place.

In a culture of money, that which can neither be bought nor sold is Holy. In countries and companies managed with predictable or even perverse power, that which erupts with the goodness of beginnings is Holy. In a society of bent purpose, that which pulls us to the point of our being is Holy. In an earth so taken for granted, those who are grateful are holy.

HOLY IS YOUR NAME
WE GIVE YOU THANKS
AND BLESS YOUR HOLY NAME

ACKNOWLEDGMENTS

Because this book was written as an act of gratitude, it seems most appropriate to acknowledge those who made it possible.

The volunteers and board members of Romero House made it possible for me to take a significant period of time away from our community of service. The Banff School of the Arts, through the Leighton Studios program for established writers, provided me with a stimulating and encouraging environment in which to write the first draft of this book.

My students at Regis College, in the University of Toronto, were willing to study this book even in draft form and provided me with fresh enthusiasm for the text. It went through many revisions and I had helpful comments from: Jack Costello S.J., Kathleen McAlpin R.S.M., Joe Hacala S.J., and Michael Creal. My neighbors, Eddy Gerek and Keith Leckie, helped solve my computer problems when I was in a pinch.

June Callwood constantly reminded me that we ought to treat one another with gratitude and kindness. My friend Lauretta Santarossa summoned me to write the prayers that are integral to this book. My agent, Lee Davis Creal, has been an enthusiastic supporter of my writing and a fine critic.

Bill Burrows and the staff of Orbis Books made this work of gratitude possible with a marvelous combination of congeniality and competence.

Finally, a word of thanks to Wilber Sutherland who was a founding member of the Sanctuary Coalition for refugees and of Imago, a foundation whose purpose is to help Christians searching for creative ways to express what it might mean to be the image of God in our world. He believed that faith and beauty and justice reflect God's great imagination of the world. A native elder from Bella Colla named him *Amtikaye: Standing on a Rock.*

NOTES ON SOURCES
AND RECOMMENDED READINGS

Chapter One: Beginnings

In this chapter, I am attempting to give expression to what the literary critic Northrop Frye called the "concern" of this culture. The South African theologian Albert Nolan, O.P., would call this the "animating question" that is reflected in all aspects of our culture. See Frye's *Divisions on a Ground* and Nolan's "Contextual Theology: One Faith, Many Theologies" (Regis College, The Chancellor's Lecture, 1990).

Throughout the world, theologians are attempting to articulate a faith that is compelling and alive within their context. The efforts of Latin American liberation theologians are perhaps the most well-known in this regard. However, I am not attempting to do a "liberation theology" for North America, as this would do justice to neither the Latin American nor the North American realities. My modest hope is to offer a preliminary and provisional outline of some of the elements to consider in developing a contextual theology in "America, the North and the West."

In thinking through the various methodological questions involved in doing contextual theology, I have relied heavily on Douglas John Hall's masterful *Thinking the Faith: Christian Theology in a North American Context* (Minneapolis: Augsburg, 1989). He relies on the "method of correlation" as it was articulated by Paul Tillich, i.e., in order to communicate with a culture you must participate in it. According to Hall, this participation does not necessarily mean relativizing the gospel. It means relating to a culture, experiencing its profound questions in order to hear the answer of the gospel anew. "The attempt to comprehend one's culture—to grasp at some depth its aspirations, its priorities, its anxieties; to discern the dominant ideational motifs of its history; to distinguish its real from its rhetorical mores—all this belongs to the theological task as such" (p. 75).

Steven Bevan's book, *Models of Contextual Theology*, is also helpful in considering questions of method. Robert Schreiter's *The New Catholicity: Globalization and the Challenge to Theology* makes the important point that we all live in multiple and overlapping contexts of meaning.

Douglas Hall and I are aware not only of significant differences between Canada and the United States but also of profound similarities. That is why in this book I have used the term "America, the North and the West" to represent something more than a geographical reality.

For an extended meditation on becoming the word that is your true self, see Thomas Merton's *New Seeds of Contemplation*. On the importance of the textuality of life (witness) in a time when authoritative texts are being called into question, see Edith Wyshygrod's *The Saints and Postmodernism*. Hannah Arendt developed a similar insight in her notion of "exemplary validity" by which a person or event exemplifies an idea that we might otherwise not be able to describe. This notion is only provisionally developed in her unfinished work, *The Life of the Mind, Volume 3: Judging*. Throughout my reflections I have taken Jesus as the "example" of radical gratitude.

Chapter Two: Perpetual Dissatisfaction

There are many articles and books on the consumer culture. Here are the ones that I have used to help me develop an understanding of the intrinsic connection between our spiritual crises and the culture of money: John Kavanaugh's now almost classic *Following Christ in a Consumer Culture*, Richard Sennett's *The Corrosion of Character: The Personal Consequences of Work in the New Capitalism*, Juliet B. Schor's *The Overworked American: The Unexpected Decline of Leisure*, Herbert Marcuse's *One-Dimensional Man: Studies in the Ideology of Advanced Industrial Society*, and Leslie Savan's *The Sponsored Life*.

While I don't entirely agree with James B. Twitchell's *Lead Us Into Temptation: The Triumph of American Materialism*, there were elements of this book that I found useful.

Wade Clark Roof has done an important study of the reconfiguration of religious and spiritual commitments taking place in North American culture in his *Spiritual Marketplace: Baby Boomers and the Remaking of American Religion.*

The story of "The House for a Car" originally appeared in my *At the Border Called Hope: Where Refugees Are Neighbors.* This story had "legs" and made its way down to an Anglican cathedral in the southwestern states where it was retold from the pulpit as an incident that had taken place between a nun and a Guatemalan woman whose husband had been killed. The Anglican priest concluded her sermon by asking, "What do you have in your garage?" One of the members of the congregation did have an expensive sports car in his garage and ended up donating it to the cathedral!

An excellent and very accessible resource on the Babylonian captivity is *Hopeful Imagination* by the scripture scholar Walter Brueggemann.

Chapter Three: Radical Gratitude

The reflections in this chapter can be situated between the two human conditions delineated by Hannah Arendt in her *The Human Condition:* the condition of natality (or birth), which gives rise to awe and amazement in classical Greek thought (*thaumazein*), and the condition of mortality (death), which is associated with the long tradition of the *vita contemplativa.*

Astonishment is articulated as the beginning of metaphysics in Martin Heidegger's *Introduction to Metaphysics* ("Why is there something rather than nothing?") and as the beginning of faith or "abiding astonishment" in Emil Fackenheim's *God's Presence in History.* For Fackenheim, the astonishment has more to do with God's initiative in history than with the creative *initio* (beginning) of the world and the human person.

In much of classical spirituality, the term "poverty of spirit" is often used as the correlative of "radical gratitude." For an excellent, although difficult, presentation of this, read *Poverty of Spirit* by Johannes B. Metz.

For the image of the morning birds that do not take the world for granted, I am indebted to Thomas Merton's description of the valley near his monastery as it awakens. See part three of *Conjectures of a Guilty Bystander.* The French philosopher Emmanuel Levinas has provided me

with the foundational insight about the importance of becoming a "guarantee" for "the other" in his monumental *Totality and Infinity*.

In my opinion, Albert Camus has crystallized the wisdom of the
West in his essay on radical gratitude in "Return to Tipasa" in his *Literary and Critical Essays*. Etty Hillesum has become the great contemporary
witness to radical gratitude, as evidenced in her diary *The Interrupted Life*.
In suggesting that the work of justice is to make the world a place in
which it is a little easier to be grateful, I have paraphrased a well-known
maxim of Peter Maurin, who, with Dorothy Day, is considered a co-
founder of the Catholic Worker movement.

My suggestion that a conversion to radical gratitude must take place
on many levels of our life draws on Bernard Lonergan's reflections on
conversion in his *Insight*. I will develop this notion further in chapter six.

In discussing the logic of scarcity (there is never enough) and the
logic of abundance (there is enough) I am drawing on a distinction found
in the works of Paul Ricoeur. See his essay, "Guilt, Ethics and Religion,"
in *The Conflict of Interpretations*.

Chapter Four: Creative Power

Some of my reflections in this chapter appeared in preliminary form
as "A Different Power," pp. 335-63 in *Women and the Holocaust: Different
Voices*, edited by Carol Rittner and John K. Roth (St. Paul, Minnesota:
Paragon Press, 1993) and as "Redeeming Power: Women in Church and
Society," Women and Christianity Lectures, St. Thomas More College,
1994.

The literature on the topic of power is voluminous. For a helpful
survey, see James Hillman's *Forms of Power* and Rollo May's *Power and Innocence*.

As far as I know, Nietzsche (*The Will to Power*) and Max Scheler
(*Ressentiment*) were the first to discuss resentment as a crucial factor in pre-
venting social or personal change. According to Nietzsche, Christianity
cultivated the resentments of the weak, whereas for Scheler, this attitude
was more indicative of how the "bourgeois spirit" had infected the church.

I am greatly indebted to Michael Lerner's early writings on powerlessness, found in his *Surplus Powerlessness*. More recently, Canadian journalist

Linda McQuaig has used the term "the cult of impotence" to describe how the myth of powerlessness serves certain interests in the global economy.

On the subject of the relationship between violence and powerlessness, see Hannah Arendt's *On Violence*. The thinking of the French anthropologist René Girard is now considered seminal on the topics of violence, scapegoating, and the sacred. His thought can be found in accessible form in Gil Baillie's *Violence Unveiled* and in Walter Wink's *Engaging the Powers*.

Concern with powerlessness is, for obvious reasons, reflected in an increasing body of feminist reflections. Some of these reflections seem to propose as an alternative a variation on the individualistic model of controlling power, including control over one's body.

Sharon D. Welch proposes a much less controlling model of power in her *A Feminist Ethic of Risk*. I found Elizabeth Janeway's book, *The Powers of the Weak*, to be a perceptive analysis of power. Carter Hayward's reflections on relational power are also helpful. See her *Our Passion for Justice*.

Although Hannah Arendt would never have called herself a feminist, she developed one of the first articulations of an interactive, intersubjective view of power in her book *The Human Condition*. This relational model is also found in the works of Martin Buber and John Macmurray's Gifford Lectures published as *The Self as Agent* and *Persons in Relation*.

The most telling comment on the shadow side of the relational model of power can be found in the works of Michel Foucault. His interviews on this subject are quite accessible in the book *Power/Knowledge*, edited by Colin Gordon.

For more practical insight into jazz as a metaphor for relational power, see *Thinking in Jazz: The Infinite Art of Improvisation*, by Paul F. Berliner. I am also grateful to Bianca Pittoors of Ottawa, who taught me a great deal about jazz at the Banff School of the Arts. For a wise guide on the practice of relational power and the interconnectedness of all being, look for just about anything by Joanna Macy (e.g., *Coming Back to Life: Practices to Reconnect Our Lives, Our World*).

In discussing the organization of power in bureaucracies and networks, I have relied heavily on Hannah Arendt's *The Origins of Totalitarianism*. The restatement of her insights in terms of contemporary organizations is chillingly presented by Earl Shorris in his *The Oppressed Middle*.

For a good account of the particular powerlessness of the middle class, see Paul King's *Social Heroism: The Middle Class and Powerlessness*. Barbara Ehrenreich has some superb insights into how the process of professionalization disempowers people. See her *The Fear of Falling: The Inner Life of the Middle Class*.

For more theological perspectives on the notion of power in the process of redemption, see: Jean Mark Laporte's *Patience and Power: Grace for the First World* and Sally B. Purvis's *The Power of the Cross*. A most satisfying discussion of the question of the omnipotence of God is found in *The Church: The Human Story of God* by Edward Schillebeeckx. He proposes that "the vulnerability of God" may be a more appropriate term than the "the powerlessness of God."

Chapter Five: The Point of Our Being

For a philosophical reflection on the collapse of religious and secular narratives, see Hannah Arendt's "The Concept of History: Ancient and Modern" in her *Between Past and Future*.

In developing my own approach to "political discernment" or "reading the signs of the times" I have used Wolfhart Pannenberg's "Dogmatic Theses on the Doctrine of Revelation," pp. 125-55 in his *Revelation as History*. In addition, I have been helped by Douglas John Hall's *Thinking the Faith*, the first volume of his trilogy on doing theology in the North American context. J. B. Metz and his reflections on *History and Society* and J. B. Libanio's work *Spiritual Discernment and Politics* have also provided me with insights.

The notion of episodic meaning is my own and I first discussed it in "Formation in the Postmodern Context," *The Way* (Summer Supplement, 1991).

My discussion of the myth of progress relies heavily on Christopher Lasch's *The True and Only Heaven: Progress and Its Critics*. John Bentley Mays' profound analysis of the twentieth century is found in his article "Picasso painting embodies legacy of the 20th century" (*Globe and Mail*, February 4, 1995, p. C18).

In assessing the situation of America in the twentieth century, I have relied on Gregory Baum's *The Twentieth Century: A Theological Overview* as well as on the writings of thinkers such as Paul Kennedy and Walter Russell Mead. I first discussed the thinkers of the "school of decline" in chapter one of my *Reweaving Religious Life*. Don DeLillo's *Underworld* provided me with vivid images of the shadow side of contemporary history. The process of scapegoating has been a major focus of much of the work of René Girard. It has been represented in a more contemporary form by Gil Baillie in *Violence Unveiled* and by James Allison in *Raising Abel*.

I have relied heavily on Barbara Ehrenreich's analysis of how the middle class experiences the future. See her *The Fear of Falling: The Inner Life of the Middle Class*.

Chapter Six: Living with Spirit

It will be obvious that I am drawing on the Aristotelian-Thomistic school of ethics in emphasizing the importance of "practices" or "habits" of gratitude.

Aristotle's approach is outlined in his *Nicomachean Ethics*, especially Books I, VIII, and IX. Thomas Aquinas builds on this approach in his *Summa Theologica* I-II.

For a helpful commentary on Aristotle, see Nancy Sherman's *The Fabric of Character: Aristotle's Theory of Virtue*. Paul J. Wadell is considered a good reference on this aspect of Aquinas's thought. See his *Friends of God: Virtues and Gifts in Aquinas* and his essay, "The Role of Charity in the Moral Theology of Thomas Aquinas," in *Aquinas and Empowerment: Classical Ethics for Ordinary Lives*, edited by G. Simon Harak, S.J. In this essay, Wadell observes that "if grace is a gift it is also a *habitus*, a new way of life constituted by distinctive practices. Those practices must be learned; indeed they require considerable training, but their transformative effects are stunning."

Stanley Hauerwas has provided a contemporary restatement of this emphasis on the formation of habits in his *Vision and Virtue: Towards an Ethics of Character*.

For a very interesting recent application of this approach as it pertains to young Christians in North America, consult the website of the Valparaiso Project.

Some specific references: Martin Buber's thoughts on holding oneself in readiness can be found in the introduction to his *The Eclipse of God*. Vaclav Havel's presentation of the importance of a "parallel culture" is in his essay "Power and Powerlessness" in *Living in Truth*. See my essay, "Doing Theology in a Parallel Culture," in *Light Burdens, Heavy Blessings*, edited by Mary Heather MacKinnon, Moni McIntyre, and Mary Ellen Sheehan. Gil Baillie's insights into imitation are found in his *Violence Unveiled*. Thomas Merton's description of the suffering of the cosmic Christ is from his *New Seeds of Contemplation*.

My indebtedness to Wendell Berry will be evident throughout this chapter and, indeed, throughout the book. His statement on "the beloved country" is in his *Standing By Words*. His criticism of the problem of thinking globally is in his *Sex, Economy, Freedom and Community*. The poem is from his *The Timbered Choir*.